MY SHEEP FOLLOW ME

A Study of Perseverance and the Threat of Antinomianism

JONATHAN R. PRATT

My Sheep Follow Me: A Study of Perseverance and the Threat of Antinomianism

Published by Kregel Academic, an imprint of Kregel Publications, 2450 Oak Industrial Dr. NE, Grand Rapids, MI 49505-6020

Cataloging-in-Publication data is available from the Library of Congress.

ISBN 978-0-8254-4936-9

Printed in the United States of America

26 27 28 29 30 / 5 4 3 2 1

"Jonathan Pratt has written a significant study on the doctrine of perseverance. The first half of his book provides a helpful overview of the doctrine as it is understood in mainstream Reformed theology. The second half reviews the development of the antinomian alternative to perseverance, then examines three contemporary movements that modify or reject the doctrine of perseverance: Free Grace, Radical Grace, and Hyper-Grace. The first half of the book is an excellent introduction to the issues, and the second half is a significant original contribution. Christian leaders who want to understand perseverance will do well to read this book."

—Kevin Bauder
Research Professor of Systematic Theology
Central Baptist Theological Seminary

"A believer's walk with God is a long journey into eternity. It is a walk of faith, and that faith abides and perseveres. This useful and focused study considers how perseverance differs from assurance and eternal security, as well as how it calls us to holiness. The study also warns of the lack of balance in some teaching that minimizes perseverance and emphasizes grace at the expense of persevering. It is a welcome reminder of an aspect of our calling to journey in the direction God leads us, as he makes us into his likeness."

—Darrell L. Bock
Senior Research Professor of NT Studies
Dallas Theological Seminary

"Not only has Dr. Pratt written a book that combines biblical and historical teaching on sanctification, but also he writes in a heartwarming manner whereby the reader is acutely aware that emphasizing grace doesn't require us to become antinomians. There's a lovely simplicity to this work, which is not easy to do when writing on this topic. A work that anyone in the church can benefit from."

—Mark Jones
Senior Minister, Faith Vancouver Presbyterian Church (PCA)

"Jon Pratt's book accomplishes two important tasks for Christians. First, it provides a summary formulation of the gospel's teachings concerning a Christian's persevering faith in Christ Jesus. Pratt emphasizes the essential need for Christians to hold in proper balance two gospel truths: (1) that all authentic believers in Jesus Christ endure in faith and obedience unto the end of their earthly lives; and (2) that believers persevere in faith by heeding the several means of grace provided by our Lord, including the gospel's numerous warnings and admonitions. Second, the book exposes three influential contemporary movements among evangelicals that advocate distorted and imbalanced beliefs concerning the teachings of Jesus and his apostles on the necessity of faith's endurance. With essentially the same motives but with slight variations, advocates of all three errors exaggerate the inevitable salvation of believers and minimize, even eliminate, the gospel's numerous warnings and admonitions to persevere in faithfulness to Christ Jesus."

—Ardel Caneday
Retired Professor of Biblical and Theological Studies
Teaching Elder, Christ Bible Church, Roseville, MN
Coauthor with Tom Schreiner of *The Race Set Before Us*

"Jon Pratt is a reliable guide to explain what the Bible teaches about progressive sanctification and to evaluate ways that well-intentioned teachers have recently deviated from sound teaching."

—Andy Naselli
Professor of Systematic Theology and New Testament
Bethlehem College and Seminary
Lead Pastor, Christ the King Church, Stillwater, MN

"Pratt explains well in this work the biblical understanding of perseverance and the liabilities of antinomianism. He conducts a helpful survey of various antinomian positions, critiquing them from a biblical standpoint. Readers desiring a clear understanding of perseverance, sanctification, and holiness will profit from this helpful work."

—Tom Schreiner
Professor of New Testament
The Southern Baptist Theological Seminary

I gratefully dedicate this book to the three people who have best modeled persevering faith to me: my parents, Ray and Marie Pratt, and my best friend and loving wife, Elaine.

CONTENTS

ABBREVIATIONS

AB	Anchor Bible
BSac	*Bibliotheca Sacra*
CTQ	*Concordia Theological Quarterly*
DBSJ	*Detroit Baptist Seminary Journal*
EuroJTh	*European Journal of Theology*
GDJT	*Gloria Deo Journal of Theology*
GTJ	*Grace Theological Journal*
JBL	*Journal of Biblical Literature*
JETS	*Journal of the Evangelical Theological Society*
JGES	*Journal of the Grace Evangelical Society*
JMAT	*Journal of Ministry and Theology*
JOT	*Journal of Translation*
NAC	New American Commentary
NICNT	New International Commentary on the New Testament
PNTC	Pillar New Testament Commentary
Presb	*Presbyterion*
ProEccl	*Pro Ecclesia*
Them	*Themelios*
TMSJ	*The Master's Seminary Journal*
TNTC	Tyndale New Testament Commentary
TrinJ	*Trinity Journal*
WBC	Word Biblical Commentary
WCF	Westminster Confession of Faith

PREFACE

The book you are about to read has been a labor of love for nearly thirty years. My interest in the subject of perseverance can be best described by using Jesus's analogy of the growing seed in Mark 4:26–28 (from the seed, to the blade, to the ear, to the full grain in the ear). The seed for this project began when I wrote a paper on Romans 6:21 for Darrell Bock during my doctoral studies at Dallas Theological Seminary. That seed developed into the blade of the plant when I penned my doctoral dissertation entitled, "The Relationship between Justification and Sanctification in Romans 5–8." I am so grateful for my supervisor for this project, John Grassmick, who provided insightful and expert guidance. Ten years later that dissertation was condensed into an article published in *Themelios*.

I acknowledge that this plant has been an extremely slow-growing one; it took another ten years for the stalk (ear) to develop as I delivered the MacDonald Lectures in 2019 at Central Baptist Theological Seminary, where I have taught New Testament and Greek since 2008. The lectures were entitled, "Issues in Sanctification," and many of the themes I covered then now appear here in more mature (I trust) formulation. Finally, the full head of grain made its appearance as I presented several papers from 2019 to 2023 at the Bible Faculty Summit, a small colloquium of Bible colleges and seminaries that meets every summer. Three of those presentations became essays published in *Detroit Baptist Seminary Journal*, *Gloria Deo Journal of Theology*, and a festschrift in honor of Larry Pettegrew. Portions of these papers appear here as chapters 7–9 with their permission.

I would like to express my heartfelt appreciation to Kregel for entrusting this work to me. In particular, the help I have received from Kristina Vandiver, Shawn Vander Lugt, and Russ Meek has been invaluable, resulting in a much-improved product.

Furthermore, my wife, Elaine, reads and helpfully comments on everything I write, and this book is no exception. Several others have read all or portions of the manuscript and provided useful insights. These include Greg Deckert, David Kowalski, Bob Meredith, Luke Miller, Ray Pratt, and Matt Shrader. The quality of this book owes much to these who have aided me, and any shortcomings rest entirely with me.

Most significantly, I offer my thanks and praise to the Lord, who by his kind and gracious power has helped me to persevere in the writing and researching of this book. But in a more substantial way, my Good Shepherd has proven faithful to his word, causing me to hear his voice and to follow him—thanks be to God!

CHAPTER 1

INTRODUCTION

In baseball, the difference between a coach and a player is quite simple: the coach explains how a curveball should be thrown, and the player actually performs the feat. In a sense the coach answers the "how" question ("How do I throw a curveball?"), and the player demonstrates the "what" question ("What does a curveball look like?"). While sanctification is *not* a game, Christians often ask the "how" question: "How do I grow in my walk with Christ?"[1] But the "what" question—"What does growth in holiness look like?"—is often overlooked or avoided.

This book addresses that second question. But we have to answer the first, the question of *method* in sanctification, prior to dealing with the second, the question about the *demonstration* of sanctification.

METHOD IN SANCTIFICATION

How does a Christian grow? While theologians are often accused of asking questions very few care about, I am confident that every believer in Jesus has made this query at one time or another. This question never occurred to me personally until my college years, when my best friend, Greg, raised the issue directly in one of our many theological discussions. Growing up in a God-honoring,

1. I am using the term *sanctification* in the commonly understood way of growth in holiness. Theologians typically describe sanctification in terms of three tenses. First, *past sanctification* refers to the definitive break from the ruling power of sin that takes place at the moment of salvation (Acts 20:32; 1 Cor 6:11; Col 3:12). Past sanctification speaks of a forensic setting apart to holiness, delivering the believer from the *penalty* of sin. Second, *present* or *progressive sanctification* speaks of the believer's process of growth throughout his earthly life; in other words, the believer's progressive deliverance from the *power* of sin (Heb 12:14; 1 John 3:3). Third, *future* or *perfected sanctification* describes the consummation of the process of sanctification when believers are made perfect (Heb 12:23) and freed from the *presence* of sin (1 Thess 3:13) at their glorification.

church-attending, gospel-loving home, the great concern of my parents, children's church workers, and pastors was that I would be saved and come to embrace Christ as the only Savior from sin. And as a young boy of five, I called on the name of the Lord and was gloriously saved. For my next fifteen years, the two main questions I heard from spiritual leaders were "Have you trusted in Christ?" and "Are you sure you have?"

Occasionally, evangelists and chapel speakers at the Bible college I attended would ask a third question: "Have you dedicated/surrendered your life to the Lord?" Maybe this is why Greg's question ("How does a Christian grow?") caught me off guard. I had never thought about it, so I gave him the only answer I knew: "You need to dedicate/surrender your life to Christ." His next question left me speechless: "Then what?"

That question set me on a quest to find an answer. My initial explanation included what I call the "two-step solution": (1) surrender/dedicate your life to Christ as Lord, and (2) follow the commands given by Christ and his apostles. Little did I realize at the time that many Christian teachers hold to some form of the "two-step solution" and that only one sanctification model—the Reformed view—actually suggests that only one step is necessary in the believer's goal of growing in the walk of faith.

Following the pattern first laid out in *Five Views on Sanctification*, there are generally five schools of sanctification teaching: Wesleyan, Keswick, Pentecostal, Chaferian, and Reformed.[2] Each of these views has particular points of emphasis, especially related to the initiation of sanctification (i.e., does God begin his work of producing fruit imme-

---

2. Melvin Dieter, ed., *Five Views on Sanctification* (Grand Rapids: Zondervan Academic, 1987). This book uses these five categories but labels one the "Augustinian-Dispensational View." This unhelpful label used by John F. Walvoord, who penned that chapter, was called the "Chaferian" view by Charles Ryrie, "Contrasting Views on Sanctification," in *Walvoord: A Tribute*, ed. Donald K. Campbell (Chicago: Moody Press, 1982), 189–200. This is the preferable term. For helpful diagrams of these models, see Andrew D. Naselli, *No Quick Fix: Where Higher Life Theology Came From, What It Is, and Why It's Harmful* (Bellingham, WA: Lexham Press, 2017), 7–27. Another excellent historical survey is found in William W. Combs, "The Disjunction Between Justification and Sanctification in Contemporary Evangelical Theology," *DBSJ* 6 (2001): 17–33.

A year after *Five Views* came out, *Christian Spirituality: Five Views of Sanctification*, ed. Donald L. Alexander (Downers Grove, IL: InterVarsity Press, 1988) was published. It differed from its predecessor by including the Lutheran view (by Gerhard O. Forde) and the contemplative view (by E. Glenn Hinson) instead of the Chaferian and Keswick views. Dieter's volume is preferred because the Lutheran view is not distinct enough from the Reformed view to merit a separate treatment and because the contemplative view is too enigmatic to be considered as a distinct view.

diately after regeneration, or does he wait for humans to begin the process?) and the degree to which God and people are involved in their ongoing growth. I will discuss each of these viewpoints by giving a short history of their origins and then outlining the significant emphases of each with particular attention to that same basic question: How do we grow spiritually?

WESLEYAN TEACHING

John Wesley (1703–1791) was the first to separate justification from sanctification, suggesting that both are received in distinct acts of faith.[3] In other words, he taught that believers are justified by faith, and then at a point in time subsequent to justification, they are sanctified by faith. Wesley's book *A Plain Account of Christian Perfection* outlines five specific elements of what he calls "entire sanctification" or "perfection": It (1) is instantaneous; (2) is distinctly subsequent to justification; (3) is only received by those who seek for it; (4) defines sin as "conscious, deliberate acts"; and (5) may be lost.[4]

Two comments are in order for understanding Wesley's teachings about perfection. First, Wesley's Arminian theology leaves the decision to be sanctified (and justified) up to the individual because all people have the moral freedom to choose due to prevenient grace.[5] This perspective means that a Christian can choose not to be sanctified as well.[6] Second, Wesley defines sin as "a voluntary transgression of a known law." Christians can be entirely sanctified because they can avoid committing voluntary sin (i.e., a "breach of the law of love").[7]

3. Much of the bibliographic details of Wesley's theological perspective can be found in Naselli, *No Quick Fix*, 8–10, and Jonathan R. Pratt, "The Relationship between Justification and Spiritual Fruit in Romans 5–8," *Them* 34 (2009): 163.
4. John Wesley, *A Plain Account of Christian Perfection* (London: J. Paramore, 1785), 22–26, 29, 36, 39, 95–97.
5. See William W. Combs, "Does the Bible Teach Prevenient Grace?" *DBSJ* 10 (2005): 3–18; and Thomas R. Schreiner, "Does Scripture Teach Prevenient Grace in the Wesleyan Sense?" in *Still Sovereign: Contemporary Perspectives on Election, Foreknowledge, and Grace*, ed. Thomas R. Schreiner and Bruce A. Ware (Grand Rapids: Baker Academic, 2000), 229–46.
6. Wesley also taught that believers can choose not to be justified after making the choice to be saved. In this he was consistently following the Arminian belief that Christians can lose their salvation.
7. John Wesley, *The Works of John Wesley*, 3rd ed., 14 vols. (1872; repr., Grand Rapids: Baker Academic, 1978), 11:396; 12:394. Wesley refused to use the phrase *sinless perfection* because he recognized that all people commit involuntary transgressions (though as indicated he does not refer to such transgressions as "sin").

Thus, for the Wesleyan, one's spiritual growth occurs through an act of faith so that the Christian experiences a "full salvation from all our sins—from pride, self-will, anger, unbelief; or, as the Apostle [Paul] expresses it, 'going on to perfection.' But what is perfection? The word has various senses: here it means perfect love. It is love excluding sin; love filling the heart, taking up the whole capacity of the soul."[8] This quotation uses language typical of the Wesleyan understanding of sanctification, and it is important to note that Wesley believed such sanctification to be impossible before the definitive act of faith, separate from the act of justifying faith, by the believer to initiate the growth process.

PENTECOSTAL TEACHING

Several theological strands contribute to the Pentecostal rope, including Wesleyan perfectionism, the holiness movement, and higher life theology as demonstrated in the writings of A. B. Simpson, D. L. Moody, and R. A. Torrey.[9] Wesley's emphasis on entire sanctification became the focal point of the holiness movement. The leaders of the movement developed this concept by connecting Spirit baptism with entire sanctification and by stressing that a crisis experience was necessary to receive or attain this Spirit baptism. How would someone know that they had received the Spirit baptism? This question was answered on December 31, 1900, when Agnes Ozman began speaking in tongues as she received Spirit baptism. To this day those who hold to Pentecostal theology believe that one must give initial evidence of their reception of Spirit baptism by speaking in tongues. Once believers receive Spirit baptism, they are enabled to grow in sanctification.

In the first decade of Pentecostalism, its leaders debated the timing of Spirit baptism and the crisis experience of entire sanctification. Some equated these events (non-holiness Pentecostals), while others separated the events, placing entire sanctification prior to Spirit baptism (holiness Pentecostals).[10] But both groups agree that: (1) baptism in the Spirit is an event distinct from and subsequent to justification, (2)

8. Wesley, *Works of Wesley*, 6:46.
9. Naselli, *No Quick Fix*, 20.
10. Stanley M. Horton, "The Pentecostal Perspective," in Dieter, *Five Views on Sanctification*, 105–9. Non-holiness Pentecostals include denominations like the Assemblies of God, while holiness Pentecostals include denominations like the Church of God (Cleveland, TN) and the Pentecostal Holiness Church.

baptism in the Spirit empowers the individual to serve obediently, and (3) baptism in the Spirit is a blessing that all believers should seek.

KESWICK TEACHING

Following a series of meetings designed to promote holiness begun during D. L. Moody's 1873 campaign in London, a pastor from the lake district in the northwest part of England, T. D. Harford-Battersby, and his Quaker friend, Robert Wilson, decided to begin a convention to promote holiness teaching in their town, Keswick. The first meeting was held in 1875, and the Keswick Convention has met every year since then. In its first generation (1875–1920), the Keswick Convention promoted its unique form of higher life theology, with many people from various denominations participating in the annual event. Each speaker during those early days of the convention was marked by their entrance into "the life of faith" when they "let go and let God" so that they were no longer "carnal" but "spiritual" Christians.[11]

Keswick teaching did not stay confined to England. Many of the early conventions promoted Keswick's higher life theology in America as well (e.g., Moody's Northfield conferences and McQuilkin's "American Keswick" conferences). Naselli suggests (rightly) that Keswick teaching spawned four institutions/movements in America, including the Christian and Missionary Alliance denomination, Moody Bible Institute, Pentecostalism, and Dallas Theological Seminary.[12]

It will be easiest to trace Keswick teaching about sanctification by looking at each of the five days of the Keswick convention's teaching plan.[13] Day one emphasizes sin and the Christian need to measure up to God's standard of holiness. Keswick teachers emphasize the importance of "counteraction" in which the "law of the Spirit of life" (Rom 8:2) counteracts the "law of sin" (Rom 7:23) in the believer's life. If the believer allows the Spirit to do his work of counteracting the sinful nature, then the Christian can live without known sin, though he or she will not be sinlessly perfect in this life.

---

11. Naselli, *No Quick Fix*, 14.
12. Naselli, *No Quick Fix*, 18. The emphasis here is on the *beginning* of these movements. The CMA, Moody Bible Institute, and Dallas Theological Seminary do not necessarily promote higher life teaching today.
13. J. Robertson McQuilkin, "The Keswick Perspective," in Dieter, *Five Views of Sanctification*, 154–56, uses this methodology to describe Keswick theology. Also see Naselli, *No Quick Fix*, 29–44.

Day two provides teaching about the cure for sin, which is the provision for the victorious life. Fundamental to this teaching about the victorious life is the Keswick understanding that there are two categories of Christians: the carnal and the spiritual.[14] The way to advance the carnal to the spiritual category is to receive the crisis, or "second blessing." At this point it will be helpful to delineate Keswick's view of sanctification's basis, nature, means, result, and agent.

1. The *basis* for sanctification is union with Christ, and the key text that points to this is Romans 6. This is a positional truth that makes it possible for all believers to live the victorious Christian life.
2. The *nature* of sanctification is threefold: gift, crisis, and process. Sanctification is a *gift* received with the *crisis* experience, which is needed to enact the process. Presenting oneself in consecration (Rom 6:13, 16, 19; 12:1) is a one-time act of yielding but must be practiced repeatedly in the Christian's life.
3. The *means* of sanctification is appropriating—i.e., choosing to make use of the gift by faith alone—not by effort or struggle.
4. The *result* of sanctification is spiritual power to serve.
5. The *agent* of sanctification is the Holy Spirit.[15]

Day three is the time when the crisis of consecration becomes the experience of the believer so that the process of sanctification can follow. The conditions for this crisis are surrender ("let go") and faith ("let God").[16] The believer must rest and trust in God's power to keep

14. Common phrases used to describe the carnal Christian include: free from sin's penalty, first stage, constant defeat, life in the flesh, Christ is Savior, out of fellowship/communion with God, self-life, spiritual bondage, virtual fruitlessness, and life of struggle/works. Common phrases used to describe the spiritual Christian include: free from sin's power, second stage, constant victory, life in the Spirit, Christ is Savior and Lord, in fellowship/communion with God, Christ-life, spiritual liberty, abundant fruitfulness, life/rest of faith. See the helpful chart in Naselli, *No Quick Fix*, 32–33.
15. Naselli, *No Quick Fix*, 35–39.
16. Common terms or phrases used to describe the act of consecration include: reckon, cooperate, hand over, consent to die, deny self, dedicate to God, terminate the self-life, abiding, and surrender by faith. These phrases come from Steven Barabas, *So Great Salvation: The History and Message of the Keswick Convention* (Westwood, NJ: Revell, 1952), 89–144. Barabas provides the best systematization of Keswick theology up until Naselli's *No Quick Fix*. Barabas's treatment was sympathetic to Keswick teaching and was positively received by Keswick teachers. On the other hand, Naselli's work is not sympathetic.

one from sin. Victory comes immediately following one's consecration—the victorious life occurs instantaneously.

Day four speaks to the need for Spirit-filling. Believers are encouraged to learn how to continue being Spirit-filled, since this is the only way to avoid relapsing into the carnal Christian state. Only consecrated Christians can be Spirit-filled, so constant vigilance is required to maintain one's Spirit-filling.

Day five provides encouragement to serve God with power, especially by evangelizing non-Christians at home and abroad. While the fifth day's spotlight on service was not part of the original convention gatherings, it eventually became the "hallmark of the Keswick Convention," with its strong emphasis on missions and world evangelization.[17]

To summarize, Keswick teaching asserts that there are two categories of Christians: the carnal and the spiritual. The way for Christians to enter the spiritual stage is by the crisis experience of consecration, which happens instantaneously, followed by the process of sanctification. Christians maintain this sanctified condition by allowing the Holy Spirit to fill them, resulting in spiritual power for service.

CHAFERIAN TEACHING

This view traces its origins to the teaching of Lewis Sperry Chafer, founder and first president of Dallas Theological Seminary (originally Evangelical Theological College; Chafer served as president from 1924–1952). His student, John Walvoord (the second president of Dallas Seminary, from 1952–1986), continued to advance Chafer's sanctification teaching.[18] This is why scholars have referred to this model of sanctification as "The Dallas Seminary Theology."[19] But Charles Ryrie, himself a student of Walvoord, referred to this model of sanctification as "Chaferian," so most have acquiesced to Ryrie's

---

17. McQuilkin, "Keswick Perspective," 155–56. Notably, thousands volunteered for missionary service as a result of the convention.
18. John Walvoord, *The Holy Spirit*, 3rd ed. (Grand Rapids: Zondervan, 1958). See especially idem, "The Augustinian-Dispensational View," in Dieter, *Five Views on Sanctification*, 199–226. This title is confusing because most would agree that the system of sanctification that Walvoord delineated was based on neither Augustine nor dispensationalism. In this regard see Jonathan Pratt, "Dispensational Sanctification: A Misnomer," *DBSJ* 7 (2002): 95–108; and Mark Snoeberger, "Second-Blessing Models of Sanctification and Early Dallas Dispensationalism," *TMSJ* 15 (2004): 93–105.
19. Combs, "Disjunction," 28.

more helpful label, especially since Dallas Seminary never claimed to hold an official position on this question.[20] Both Ryrie and Dwight Pentecost, another student of Walvoord's, have written in support of the Chaferian model.[21]

While some might suggest that Chaferian teaching is just a subset of Keswick teaching, its teachers would disagree, arguing that there are enough differences to merit a separate category. Before spelling out these differences, it will be helpful to discuss the points of emphasis found in the Chaferian model of sanctification. First, the human race is divided into three distinct categories: the natural (unconverted), the carnal (saved but unconverted in lifestyle), and the spiritual (saved and Spirit-filled). Thus, there are two classes of Christians: the *carnal*, who walk in accordance with the flesh, and the *spiritual*, who walk in accordance with the Spirit (i.e., who are filled with the Spirit).[22] Second, the means to victory over the carnal nature is yieldedness to the Holy Spirit[23] (also referred to as "dedication" or "surrender" of one's life).[24] This is viewed as a one-time decision (based on the idea that in Greek the aorist tense speaks of point-in-time action—an idea that has been discredited[25]), and it is a decision that bears immediate results—real spiritual progress can now begin. It is also important that Christians exercise continued vigilance to maintain the filling of the Spirit by keeping from quenching the Spirit by being unyielding to the will of God. Third, Chaferians separate justification and sanctification by stressing the significance of accepting Christ only as Savior, an action that saves a person. Then, at a point subsequent to one's justification, a Christian must accept Christ as Lord so that the process of sanctification can begin. In Ryrie's chapter entitled, "Must Christ Be Lord to Be Savior?" he states,

20. Ryrie, "Contrasting Views," 189–200.
21. Ryrie, "Contrasting Views"; idem, *Balancing the Christian Life* (Chicago: Moody, 1969); and J. Dwight Pentecost, *Designed to be Like Him: Fellowship, Conduct, Conflict, Maturity* (Chicago: Moody, 1966).
22. Lewis Sperry Chafer, *He That Is Spiritual* (1918; repr. Grand Rapids: Zondervan Academic, 1964), 3, 13, 39.
23. Chafer, *Spiritual*, 40; Walvoord, "Augustinian-Dispensational Perspective," 220.
24. Ryrie, *Balancing*, 186; Walvoord, *The Holy Spirit*, 197–98.
25. Frank Stagg, "The Abused Aorist," *JBL* 91 (1972): 222–31; D. A. Carson, *Exegetical Fallacies*, 2nd ed. (Grand Rapids: Baker Academic, 1996), 68–73; and Constantine R. Campbell, *Basics of Verbal Aspect in Biblical Greek*, 2nd ed. (Grand Rapids: Zondervan Academic, 2024), 88–101.

> The importance of this question cannot be overestimated in relation to both salvation and sanctification. The message of faith only and the message of faith plus commitment of life cannot both be the gospel; therefore, one of them is a false gospel and comes under the curse of perverting the gospel or preaching another gospel (Gal 1:6–9), and this is a very serious matter. As far as sanctification is concerned, if only committed people are saved people, then where is there room for carnal Christians?[26]

These three aspects of the Chaferian model share many similarities with Keswick teaching, but there are at least three ways the two models differ and thus merit separate treatments. First, the one-time act of dedication or Spirit-filling is not to be equated with second blessing or higher life theology, which suggests a Christian may be able to reach a state of perfection.[27] Second, the Chaferian model explains the experience of growing in holiness following the one-time decision of dedication in the same terms as the Reformed view of sanctification, in which both God and the believer are involved in the process of sanctification. The Keswick view, however, stresses a quietism on the believer's part.[28] Third, Ryrie argues that both the Chaferian and Reformed views tie justification and sanctification together: "The Reformed view considers justification and sanctification inseparable yet distinct, whereas the Chaferian view sees justification and sanctification as distinct, yet inseparable. In contrast to both of those, the Victorious Life view [Keswick view] understands justification and sanctification to be separate and distinct."[29] While I agree with Ryrie's assessment of the Keswick view, the Chaferian view is not as close to the Reformed view as he suggests.[30]

---

26. Ryrie, *Balancing*, 170. One can see the seriousness of the rhetoric in this quotation, which is part of the reason why the Lordship controversy of the late '80s became so heated.
27. Chafer, *Spiritual*, 41.
28. Ryrie, "Contrasting Views," 196; Robert N. Wilkin, "We Believe In: Sanctification. Part 3: Present Sanctification: God's Role in Present Sanctification," *JGES* 7 (1994): 9.
29. Ryrie, "Contrasting Views," 194.
30. Combs, "Disjunction," 30, gives a number of statements from Chaferian authors that prove the Chaferian view to be much more similar to the Keswick view than to the Reformed view, particularly in regard to the need for a specific act of surrender in order to receive Spirit-filling, "Until the believer has experienced this single, one-time act of dedication, he may be justified, but there can be no real spiritual progress—no sanctification." Randall Gleason, "B. B. Warfield and Lewis S. Chafer on Sanctification," *JETS* 40 (1997): 251, agrees: "Insisting on the absolute necessity of such dedication if a believer is to experience victory over sin while suggesting a time interval between the believer's conversion and his

In summary, the two aspects of Chaferian teaching that distinguish it from Keswick theology both relate to the nature of a post-dedication experience: it is not perfectionistic and it sees the need for the believer's active participation in the process of sanctification.

REFORMED TEACHING

While each of the four views already presented differ in significant ways from each other, all are rightly concerned with personal holiness. In fact, these models seek to exalt Christ, are warmly devotional, emphasize spiritual disciplines, affirm fundamental orthodoxy, and have a legacy of faithful Christian leaders.[31] With regard to their desire to win the fight against sin in the battle for holiness, however, they have all "taken a wrong turn into John Wesley's laboratory" and adopted an unbiblical disjunction between justification and progressive sanctification.[32]

Arising from the teachings of the sixteenth-century reformers, the Reformed view has consistently affirmed the connection between justification and sanctification, arguing that Christians will necessarily and inevitably grow in their walk of faith once they have been saved. For example, John Calvin states, "Man is justified by faith alone . . . ; nevertheless[,] actual holiness of life, so to speak, is not separated from free imputation of righteousness."[33] A. A. Hodge states that "the instant [the believer] acts [exercises] faith in Christ he is justified, and sanctification, which is the work of carrying on and perfecting that which is begun in regeneration, is accomplished under the conditions of those new relations into which he is introduced by justification."[34] And B. B. Warfield adds, "The whole sixth chapter of Romans, for example, was written for no other purpose than to assert and demonstrate that justification and sanctification are indissolubly bound together."[35]

---

arrival at this state of yieldedness draws a temporal distinction between justification and progressive sanctification. Such a two-stage, crisis-oriented view of sanctification stands in sharp contrast to the unity of salvation that Warfield emphasized."

31. Naselli, *No Quick Fix*, 45–46.
32. This descriptive turn of phrase comes from Combs, "Disjunction," 33.
33. John Calvin, *Institutes of the Christian Religion*, ed. John T. McNeill, trans. Ford Lewis Battles (Philadelphia: Westminster, 1960), 3.3.1.
34. A. A. Hodge, *Outlines of Theology*, rev. ed. (1878; repr., Grand Rapids: Eerdmans, 1928), 522.
35. B. B. Warfield, *Perfectionism*, ed. Samuel G. Craig (Grand Rapids: Baker Academic, 1958), 356.

The Reformed view emphasizes the work of God, who is the primary impetus behind the believer's growth in obedience. The Holy Spirit is God's agent in motivating the believer to live obediently. Believers do play a part, then, in their growth, but always and only in light of the Spirit's work in them. Jerry Bridges summarizes this concept well: "Though it is the Spirit who enables us to put to death our corruptions, yet Paul says this is our action as well. The very same work is from one point of view the work of the Spirit, and from another the work of man."[36]

In summary, the Reformed view emphasizes the work of God in causing believers to act obediently. The Christian does participate in the development of this obedience but only by means of the guiding ministry of the indwelling Holy Spirit. Since God is so closely involved in the process, the believer will "certainly or necessarily give evidence of an obedient lifestyle."[37]

I believe that the Reformed model best answers the "how" question of sanctification.[38] But this is only the first of the two questions raised at the beginning of this chapter. The second relates to the "what" of sanctification.

DEMONSTRATION OF SANCTIFICATION

My experience of hearing preachers stress the surrender/dedication issue with regard to sanctification pushed me to pursue the "how" question. But hardly any I knew asked the "what" question: "Are you bearing any spiritual fruit?" or "Are you acting like a Christian?" This is the question of perseverance and the focal point of this book. First, though, we must define perseverance.

The Meaning of Perseverance

Typically, a biblical-theological study proceeds inductively by looking at the texts in Scripture that speak to the theme or doctrine being studied and then providing a summary explanation of that doctrine. In the present case, however, I need to distinguish between the meanings of three often-confused terms—perseverance, preservation (eternal security), and assurance—to avoid a confusion of categories.

36. Jerry Bridges, *The Pursuit of Holiness* (Colorado Springs: NavPress, 1978), 81.
37. Pratt, "Relationship between Justification and Spiritual Fruit," 163.
38. Knowledge of these five models will prove helpful when we consider the subject matter of chapters 7–9.

Perseverance

The Westminster Confession of Faith (17.1) explains perseverance in this way: "They whom God hath accepted in His Beloved, effectually called and sanctified by His Spirit, can neither totally or finally fall away from the state of grace, but shall certainly persevere therein to the end, and be eternally saved." Put more succinctly, true believers will continue in faith and good works to the end of their earthly lives—every true Christian will produce righteous fruit. Three verses among many substantiate this truth:

- "You did not choose me, but I chose you and appointed you that you should go and bear fruit and that your fruit should abide" (John 15:16).
- "For we are his workmanship, created in Christ Jesus for good works, which God prepared beforehand, that we should walk in them" (Eph 2:10).
- "And I am sure of this, that he who began a good work in you will bring it to completion at the day of Jesus Christ" (Phil 1:6).

Preservation or Eternal Security

Preservation is the objective truth that God secures and guarantees the final salvation of all true believers. Simply put, God promises that salvation can never be lost. Jesus said this about his children: "My sheep hear my voice, and I know them, and they follow me. I give them eternal life, and they will never perish, and no one will snatch them out of my hand. My Father, who has given them to me, is greater than all, and no one is able to snatch them out of the Father's hand" (John 10:27–29). Paul believed that the Lord would bring him safely into his heavenly kingdom (2 Tim 4:18) and "guard until that day what [had] been entrusted to [him]" (2 Tim 1:12). Paul also said that Christ "will sustain you to the end, guiltless in the day of our Lord Jesus Christ" (1 Cor 1:8). He further points to the ministry of the Holy Spirit, who has been given to Christians as a seal or guarantee of their salvation (2 Cor 1:22; 5:5; Eph 1:13–14; 4:30) and is the firstfruits of their future glorification (Rom 8:23). Peter described our salvation as "kept in heaven" by the Father, "guarded through faith," and "prepared" or "ready" for final salvation (1 Pet 1:4–5), and Jude 1 states that Christians are "kept for Jesus Christ." Thus, the Scriptures teach that once people believe in Jesus for salvation, their future existence in heaven is eternally secure and can never be lost.[39] We can truly say that once someone has been justified, they cannot and will not ever lose their salvation; they are eternally preserved and secure in Christ.

Some theologians have mistakenly treated perseverance and preservation as synonyms,[40] so clarifications are in order. First, *preservation* refers to God's power to preserve or keep a person who has believed in Christ for eternal life. On the other hand, *perseverance* refers to the Christian's continuation in holiness and good works of obedience.[41] Second, "the perspective of *preservation* is from God's viewpoint. . . . A kindred doctrine, *perseverance*, looks at it from the believer's viewpoint; that is, the believer will progress in the Christian life until the day of final redemption."[42] To clarify, the actors in these two scenarios are different: regarding *preservation*, God keeps; regarding *perseverance*, the Christian obeys. Finally, consider these two ideas in terms of what they promise to keep: *preservation* means that God keeps believers in the faith (i.e., God ensures that believers will not lose their salvation); *perseverance* means that God keeps the believer in doing good works

---

39. Numerous resources have been written about preservation, so I limit reference to four: Sam Storms, *Kept for Jesus: What the New Testament Really Teaches about Assurance of Salvation and Eternal Security* (Wheaton, IL: Crossway, 2015); Robert Gromacki, *Is Salvation Forever?* (Chicago: Moody Press, 1973); J. F. Strombeck, *Shall Never Perish* (Moline, IL: Strombeck Agency, 1936); and Robert A. Peterson, "'Though All Hell Should Endeavor to Shake': God's Preservation of His Saints," *Presb* 17 (1991): 40–57.
40. John Piper, *Astonished by God: Ten Truths to Turn the World Upside Down* (Minneapolis: Desiring God, 2018), 134, states, "This doctrine, which goes by different names, has an urgent and practical application to our life together as Christians. Some call it the doctrine of eternal security. Some call it the doctrine of perseverance." The context of Piper's discussion shows that he is talking about perseverance and not eternal security (preservation), but he unhelpfully equates the two in this statement. Also see Lewis Sperry Chafer, *Systematic Theology*, 8 vols. (Dallas: Dallas Seminary Press, 1948), 3:267–354; Charles C. Ryrie, *Basic Theology* (Wheaton, IL: Victor, 1988), 328; and Henry C. Thiessen, *Lectures in Systematic Theology* (Grand Rapids: Eerdmans, 1949), 294–99. To use *preservation* as a synonym for *perseverance* is one way perseverance as defined here is misunderstood. Two other ways people may misapprehend perseverance: (1) they equate perseverance with the idea of endurance (e.g., "I persevered to the end of the hike."), or (2) they think of perseverance as the notion of bearing up under the burden of a trial (e.g., "I am asking God to help me persevere during this period of unemployment."). While these are legitimate uses of this term, it is not the way perseverance is being used in this book.
41. Robert A. Peterson, "Preservation, Perseverance, Assurance, and Apostasy," *Presb* 22 (1996): 31–33.
42. Rolland McCune, *A Systematic Theology of Biblical Christianity*, 3 vols. (Detroit: Detroit Baptist Theological Seminary, 2010), 3:159 (emphasis original).

(i.e., God ensures that believers will live obediently and bear good fruit to the end of their lives).

Assurance

Assurance is the subjective awareness or inner confidence of one's personal knowledge and certainty of eternal salvation. It is a kind of personal and emotional intuition. John describes assurance in 1 John 2:3 ("And by this we know that we have come to know him, if we keep his commandments") and in 1 John 5:13 ("I write these things . . . that you may know that you have eternal life"). Paul states, "The Spirit himself bears witness with our spirit that we are children of God" (Rom 8:16). And the author of Hebrews 6:11 desires that his readers "have the full assurance of hope until the end" even as they are to "draw near [to God] with a true heart in full assurance of faith" (Heb 10:22). The NT clearly affirms that Christians can have assurance of their salvation.[43]

Many authors have recognized that the Bible gives three foundational bases by which believers may be assured of their salvation: (1) the *promises of God* to save and keep his own, (2) the *perseverance* of the believer in good works, and (3) the *inner witness of the Holy Spirit*. The first of these is the objective ground and the latter two are the subjective grounds of assurance.[44]

Though there is little confusion regarding the differences between assurance and perseverance, people often misunderstand how they relate to each other in the believer's experience. Perhaps we could frame this discussion best with a question: Can a Christian have assurance of salvation without perseverance? Some have sought to answer this question affirmatively because they want to avoid moral-

43. All Protestants would agree with this statement. Roman Catholics, however, reject the idea that assurance is possible. See H. J. Schroeder, trans. and ed., *Canons and Decrees of the Council of Trent: English Translation* (Rockford, IL: TAN Books & Publishers, 1978), 35. Robert A. Peterson, "Christian Assurance: Its Possibility and Foundations," *Presb* 18 (1992): 10–13, gives a helpful overview of the Roman Catholic teaching on assurance.

44. WCF 18.1–2. Further discussion and commentary on this truth may be found here: Joel R. Beeke, *Knowing and Growing in Assurance of Faith* (Fearn, Ross-shire: Christian Focus, 2017), 75–120; Peterson, "Christian Assurance," 14; D. A. Carson, "Reflections on Assurance," in Schreiner and Ware, *Still Sovereign*, 275n50; Thomas R. Schreiner and Ardel B. Caneday, *The Race Set Before Us: A Biblical Theology of Perseverance and Assurance* (Downers Grove, IL: IVP Academic, 2001), 276.

ism or legalism that might result in pride or exhaustion[45] or because they want to avoid doubt and uncertainty that might cause paralyzing inertia.[46] I will argue, however, that a proper understanding of the relationship between these two doctrines is that assurance and perseverance are inseparable, and that "to stress the Word and downplay [perseverance and the inner witness of the Spirit] is to risk easy believism and antinomianism."[47] In other words, perseverance is a necessary aspect of a Christian's walk that thereby gives assurance to the one who is bearing fruit.

Stating the necessity of seeing spiritual fruit in the believer's life often leads to a question: "How much fruit is enough?" On one hand, Scripture affirms that Christians will sin (1 John 1:8–9) and that perfection is not possible on this side of glory (Heb 12:7). On the other hand, obedience is not some sort of quantifiable substance that can be weighed on a scale.[48] I believe it will be more helpful to answer this fruit-bearing question with some diagnostic questions:

- Do I care about obedience in my life?
- Do I long to please my heavenly Father?
- Do I want to love and serve Christ?
- Do I care when I stumble and sin?
- Do I confess and repent when I sin?

Answering "Yes!" to these questions is ample evidence of a regenerate heart producing fruit.

---

45. Jon Moffitt, Justin Perdue, and Jimmy Buehler, *Safe in Christ: A Primer on Assurance* (Columbia, SC: Theocast, 2020), 44–46.
46. Joseph Dillow, "Finding Assurance," in *A Defense of Free Grace Theology with Respect to Saving Faith, Perseverance, and Assurance*, ed. Fred Chay (The Woodlands, TX: Grace Theology Press, 2017), 231–32; David R. Anderson, *Free Grace Soteriology*, 3rd ed. (The Woodlands, TX: Grace Theology Press, 2018), 228.
47. Peterson, "Christian Assurance," 22. Peterson helpfully observes that when considering the three foundations of assurance, "epistemological priority must be given to the first and objective foundation—God's promises to save and keep his people. Let only those who profess faith in Christ consider the other two, subjective foundations."
48. Consider this rather absurd example: In the discussion about carnal versus spiritual Christians, if someone is able to speak truthfully at least 51 percent of the time while only lying 49 percent of the time, then we can consider him to be spiritual. But if those numbers are reversed, our friend has slipped into the carnal Christian category.

Summary

Perseverance as explained in this book mirrors Westminster Confession of Faith 17.1 and the understanding of most theologians that true believers will continue in faith and good works until the end of their earthly lives. As we shall see in the pages ahead, the Bible repeatedly affirms this.[49] We cannot, however, properly understand the doctrine of perseverance merely by observing the statements of its reality in believers' lives as seen in the Bible's indicative declarations (the assertions of its reality). No, we must also affirm the imperative statements in which the biblical writers command believers to persevere in the faith. Theologian Rolland McCune summarizes this truth well: "If it is true that a believer *will* persevere [in the faith], then it is equally true that he *must* persevere."[50] This statement suggests that there are two elements involved in perseverance—the indicative statements about the believer's progressive sanctification and growth in holiness and the imperative statements that demand the believer's obedience in the process of sanctification. In short, we must affirm both the *reality* of perseverance (the indicatives) and the *means* of perseverance (the imperatives).[51]

As with any teaching of Scripture, the doctrine of perseverance can be misunderstood, ignored, and even denied. Errors of this nature tend toward one of two poles. On one end are those who overemphasize the commands to persevere (the imperatives) and fall into the problem of legalism or moralism. On the other end of the spectrum we find

---

49. As we shall see in chapters 2–5, the biblical data supporting perseverance far outweighs that of any of the other doctrines of grace. I am not asserting that this makes it the most significant of those doctrines by virtue of its number of references alone, but I am asserting that the biblical authors believe this truth to be very important in light of its frequent mention.

50. McCune, *Systematic Theology*, 3:181 (emphasis original). Ján Henžel, "'And Grace Will Lead Me Home.' Perseverance of Believers as Divine Gift and Human Responsibility," *EuroJTh* 12 (2003): 31, states: "The perseverance of the believer is not only the divine gift of persistence in faith and the preservation of the believer to the end but also the believer's responsibility to believe and to withstand any difficulty."

51. There are several means that God uses to help his children persevere: (1) commands of Scripture, (2) suffering, (3) conditional promises/warnings, (4) Christian fellowship in the church, (5) prayer, and (6) spiritual disciplines. We will consider these means in greater detail in chapter 5.

    Any one of these means can be distorted or minimized, creating threats to perseverance. For example, prosperity gospel proponents deny that God uses suffering to produce spiritual fruit in believers' lives because they do not believe that God has anything to do with suffering. In this book we will not be considering all distortions of the means of perseverance but will zero in on one area in particular—antinomianism.

those who overemphasize the statements that believers will persevere (the indicatives) and fall into the error of antinomianism or quietism.[52] The first group focus on law and the second group focus on grace. For the first group the Christian life is all about doing, and for the second group the Christian life is all about resting or trusting.

While the message of *doing* may appeal to some Christians, especially those oriented to rule-keeping and to-do lists, the message of *resting* perpetrated by many grace teachers in our current day has far greater appeal. Those studying and teaching in this grace school are embracing an antinomian curriculum with dangerous consequences. They may be denying the importance of perseverance in order to give assurance to doubting believers or to give relief to moralistic/legalistic believers, but regardless of the motivation, they are effectively minimizing the importance of the commands of Scripture. In this way they represent a modern-day form of antinomianism. Sadly, this popular antinomian teaching has three faces or, to change the metaphor, three streams.

The evangelical antinomian river that I will describe in this book is fed by three different streams of sanctification teaching. Flowing out of the Chaferian model of sanctification we shall learn about the Free Grace antinomians. Proponents of the Reformed model have developed a stream of antinomianism called Radical Grace. Finally, the Pentecostal model has spawned the Hyper-Grace antinomians.

THE ROAD AHEAD

In this introductory chapter I have laid out the method of sanctification by considering the five models or approaches to how growth in holiness occurs. I have also presented the doctrine of perseverance, which speaks to the actual demonstration of sanctification. In order to understand what perseverance is, I have defined it and compared it to two companion doctrines, assurance and preservation/eternal security. I also have shown how the error of antinomianism has arisen due to an overemphasis of the indicatives of perseverance while minimizing the

52. Two terms in this sentence (e.g., antinomianism and error) require explanation. First, "antinomianism" means "against law" and often connotes lawless living; we will learn much more about this in chapter 6. Second, "error" refers to belief that is unhealthy and contains false doctrine, and in this book I refer to antinomianism as an error—not as dangerous as an unorthodox heresy but more perilous than a mistake or unintentional misstep.

imperatives of perseverance. In this way the reader should be prepared to follow the argument I will pursue.

Because a solid scriptural foundation of perseverance is necessary before considering any unhealthy distortion of it, we spend four chapters investigating the NT teaching about perseverance—part 1 of the book. Chapters 2–4 consider the indicatives of perseverance by examining the teachings of Jesus (chapter 2), Paul (chapter 3), and the General Epistles (chapter 4). In chapter 5 we learn the scriptural teaching regarding the means of perseverance as we study the ways by which God causes his children to bear fruit in their lives.

Once this biblical foundation has been established, part 2 (chapters 6–9) help the reader to learn about the erroneous distortion of perseverance as we consider the threat of antinomianism in the evangelical church. Chapter 6 provides a short history of antinomianism in the Christian church from 1600 to 1950. We can learn much from church history by considering how antinomianism was manifested in earlier days and how the supporters of perseverance sought to squelch its devastating effects.

I will follow the same pattern of explanation for each of the three streams of antinomianism in chapters 7–9. For each group we consider the history, proponents, and tenets embraced. Then, each chapter describes how the teaching of that group relates to the doctrine of perseverance. Finally, the reader learns how each stream connects to antinomianism as we contemplate how each group's emphases measure up to the characteristics of antinomianism discovered in chapter 6. We learn about Free Grace teaching in chapter 7. Chapter 8 investigates the Radical Grace group, and chapter 9 covers Hyper-Grace proponents.

Chapter 10 summarizes the findings from parts 1 and 2 and then provides some implications and applications for the doctrine of perseverance in the church today.

Let's start by learning from our master and teacher as we sit at his feet in chapter 2.

PART 1

SCRIPTURAL FOUNDATION

CHAPTER 2

THE TEACHING OF JESUS

"Go the 'distance.'" This is one of three whispered messages that an Iowa farmer named Ray Kinsella received in the baseball fantasy film, *Field of Dreams*. I know this is an unlikely source of a wonderful theological concept, but it certainly summarizes well the NT doctrine of perseverance, that true Christians must bear spiritual fruit to the end of their earthly lives. Alongside the imperative to bear fruit stands the equally important reality (the indicative) that Christians will bear fruit.[1]

INTRODUCTION

Part 1 of this book aims to delineate the ways that Jesus, Paul, and the writers of the General Epistles teach the biblical doctrine of perseverance and then to explain the means God uses to keep believers in persevering faith. Here are four points of clarification that will help frame the discussion for chapters 2–4.

---

1. The doctrine of perseverance is by no means a neglected doctrine as a glance at many of the church confessions shows: the Augsburg Confession (1530), §6; the Scots Confession (1560), §13; the Thirty-Nine Articles (1563), §12; the Second Helvetic Confession (1566), §114, §115, §119; WCF (1647), §17; Second London Baptist Confession (1689), §13, §17; the Articles of Religion (1784), §10; and the New Hampshire Confession (1833), §11. Note also John Jefferson Davis, "The Perseverance of the Saints: A History of the Doctrine," *JETS* 34 (June 1991): 213–28.

   Nor has it been overlooked in systematic theologies. For a thorough bibliography of important works on perseverance, see Robert A. Peterson, "Perseverance and Apostasy: A Bibliographic Essay," *Presb* 16 (1990): 119–25. Several noteworthy biblical-theological works have been written on the subject in the last sixty-five years: G. C. Berkouwer, *Faith and Perseverance*, trans. Robert D. Knudsen (Grand Rapids: Eerdmans, 1958); Judith M. Gundry Volf, *Paul and Perseverance: Staying In and Falling Away* (Louisville: Westminster John Knox, 1990); Schreiner and Caneday, *The Race Set Before Us*; Thomas R. Schreiner, *Run to Win the Prize: Perseverance in the New Testament* (Wheaton, IL: Crossway, 2010); Robert A. Peterson, "The Perseverance of the Saints: A Theological Exegesis of Four Key New Testament Passages," *Presb* 17 (1991): 95–112; and idem, "Preservation, Perseverance, Assurance, and Apostasy," 33.

First, while verses about preservation and assurance do touch in certain ways on perseverance, I am limiting this study to biblical data that directly relates to the definition of perseverance: namely, that believers will continue to the end of their earthly lives in obedience by producing righteous fruit.

Second, our study will be limited to fruit-bearing *obedience* rather than divinely bestowed *possessions*. Spiritual fruit is the righteous response of a believer to the prompting of the Holy Spirit. These righteous responses include a person's actions, attitudes, and thoughts. This evidence of spiritual fruit should be distinguished from possessions. For example, when Paul states that believers enjoy peace with God as a result of being justified in Romans 5:1, he is speaking of a *possession* believers enjoy. But this blessing does not speak to any *fruit bearing* on the believer's part. In the next two verses, we do see an action believers perform—rejoicing in hope and tribulations. This rejoicing is an example of spiritual fruit bearing—a righteous response.

Third, descriptions of persevering actions need to be presented in the indicative mood, the mood of assertion or the presentation of certainty,[2] rather than the oblique moods, which refer to actions as merely possible or commanded.[3] For example, we find a number of imperatives calling believers to live obediently, but though these are means God uses to encourage perseverance, they do not speak to the existence or nonexistence of obedient actions in the lives of those addressed.

Fourth, promises of God's persevering work on behalf of one individual (e.g., Peter in Luke 22:31–32 or Paul in 2 Tim 4:16–18) do not constitute the kind of examples we hope to unearth as we consider God's work for his people. God's ability to help individuals like Peter or Paul does not necessarily translate into promises that God will help all believers persevere.

With these restrictions established we are ready to begin by looking first at the teaching of Jesus.

---

2. Daniel B. Wallace, *Greek Grammar beyond the Basics: An Exegetical Syntax of the New Testament* (Grand Rapids: Zondervan Academic, 1996), 448.
3. The oblique moods in Greek are the subjunctive, optative, and imperative moods.

JESUS AND PERSEVERANCE

Jesus affirms the doctrine of perseverance in his teaching in at least three ways. First, he uses the metaphor of fruit bearing; second, he utilizes the metaphor of sheep; and third, he employs conditional statements.

Metaphors of Fruit Bearing

When Jesus advocates perseverance, he does so by using three distinct fruit-bearing metaphors: (1) the parable of the sower, (2) teaching about fruit-bearing trees, and (3) teaching about the vine and branches in John 15.

The parable of the sower is perhaps the most well-known parable in the Gospels (Matt 13:1–9, 18–23; Mark 4:1–20; Luke 8:5–15). It is one of the few Jesus interprets, and it appears virtually the same in all three Synoptic Gospels. Here is Mark's account:

> Listen! Behold, a sower went out to sow. And as he sowed, some seed fell along the path, and the birds came and devoured it. Other seed fell on rocky ground, where it did not have much soil, and immediately it sprang up, since it had no depth of soil. And when the sun rose, it was scorched, and since it had no root, it withered away. Other seed fell among thorns, and the thorns grew up and choked it, and it yielded no grain. And other seeds fell into good soil and produced grain, growing up and increasing and yielding thirtyfold and sixtyfold and a hundredfold. (4:3–8)

Jesus explains that the seed on the path is taken away by Satan (4:15), the rocky-soil seed falls away (4:17), and the thorny-soil seed proves unfruitful (4:19). Only the last seed, sown on good ground, produces fruit (4:20), and it is only the last soil that represents true believers.[4]

There are at least two times in Jesus's ministry when he teaches about fruit-bearing trees. In Matthew 12:33–35a Jesus discusses the good fruit that comes only from good trees. Jesus also speaks about the ability to recognize true believers on the basis of the good fruit they produce (Matt 7:15–20; Luke 6:43–45).

---

4. J. C. Ryle, *Mark: Expository Thoughts on the Gospels*, Crossway Classic Commentaries (1857; repr., Wheaton, IL: Crossway, 1993), 47–49.

Jesus's discussion of the vine and branches provides four clear statements regarding the good fruit that comes from abiding in the vine. First, Jesus says, "Every branch in me that does not bear fruit he takes away, and every branch that does bear fruit he prunes, that it may bear more fruit" (John 15:2). Two types of branches are described here: those that do not bear fruit, which are taken away, and those that bear fruit, which are pruned so that they can bear more fruit. True believers are pruned and bear fruit, and unbelievers do not bear fruit and are taken away.

Second, Jesus continues his discourse, "I am the vine; you are the branches. Whoever abides in me and I in him, he it is that bears much fruit, for apart from me you can do nothing. If anyone does not abide in me he is thrown away like a branch and withers; and the branches are gathered, thrown into the fire, and burned" (15:5–6). These verses show that: (1) good branches abide in Christ and bear much fruit, and (2) bad branches do not abide in Christ but rather wither and are thrown into the fire. These bad branches, representing unbelievers, can do nothing.[5]

Third, Jesus explains, "By this my Father is glorified, that you bear much fruit and so prove to be my disciples" (15:8). Someone demonstrates they are a disciple/believer by bearing fruit, such as believing and following his word (v. 7), obeying his commands (v. 10), and loving him and other believers (vv. 12–14).[6]

Fourth, Jesus leaves no doubt regarding believers' perseverance: "You did not choose me, but I chose you and appointed you that you should go and bear fruit and that your fruit should abide, so that whatever you ask the Father in my name, he may give it to you" (15:16). In the strongest statement of the chapter Jesus states that he has appointed his chosen ones to bear fruit and to ensure that the fruit they produce abides and continues (*menē* speaks of the idea of permanence in John, e.g., 15:10 and the continuance and permanence of the relationship between Jesus and the Father).[7]

---

5. J. Carl Laney, "Abiding Is Believing: The Analogy of the Vine in John 15:1–6," *BSac* 146 (1989): 55–66. For a contrary view, see Joseph C. Dillow, "Abiding Is Remaining in Fellowship: Another Look at John 15:1–6," *BSac* 147 (1990): 44–53.
6. Peterson, "The Perseverance of the Saints," 111.
7. Leon Morris, *The Gospel According to John*, NICNT (Grand Rapids: Eerdmans, 1971), 644, among many others.

Metaphor of Sheep

In John 10:27 we read, "My sheep hear my voice, and I know them, and they follow me." I chose this verse as the title for this book because of its straightforward declaration. Indeed, Jesus's sheep follow their master—no exceptions, no nuance, and no further explanation required.[8]

Conditional Statements

Conditional statements often share an element of contingency when the apodosis (the "then" portion of the condition) provides a possible outcome if the protasis (the "if" portion of the condition) is accomplished (e.g., "If he hits a home run, then his team will win the game"). But they can also be employed as a literary device to give factual information in that both the protasis and apodosis share equivalence when the two elements of the condition could be switched and still have the same meaning (e.g., 1 Corinthians 15:44b: "If there is a natural body, there is also a spiritual body").[9] Three conditional statements by Jesus in John's gospel stand out.

First, John 8:31–32 reads, "So Jesus said to the Jews who had believed him, 'If you abide in my word, you are truly my disciples, and you will know the truth, and the truth will set you free.'" The two elements of the condition could be reversed with the same meaning: true disciples of Jesus abide in Jesus's word. Or, to say it another way, abiding in Jesus's teaching proves that these hearers are true disciples. We learn later in the chapter that they fail to continue to follow Jesus's teaching because they do the works of the devil (8:44) and seek to stone Jesus (8:59), but true believers would never act this way.

Second, Jesus makes two more conditional statements in John 14:21–24. The first condition is implicit and could be translated, "If someone loves me, then he will be loved by my Father" (v. 21b).[10] The act of loving Jesus indicates that the person is loved by the Father, that he is a believer. Furthermore, Jesus says that such a person would also be loved by Jesus himself and that Jesus would manifest himself to that

8. McCune, *Systematic Theology,* 3:188.
9. Steve Nicolle, "Conditionals in the New Testament," *JOT* 18 (2022): 1–30; Wallace, *Greek Grammar,* 682–84; Stanley E. Porter, *Idioms of the Greek New Testament*, 2nd ed. (Sheffield: JSOT Press, 1994), 267; James L. Boyer, "First Class Conditions: What Do They Mean?" *GTJ* 2 (Spring 1981): 76.
10. Wallace, *Greek Grammar*, 688.

person. Only true believers could love Jesus, and only true believers would be loved by the Father and the Son and enjoy the manifestation of the Son to them.

The second condition in verse 23 shows that anyone who loves Jesus will be obedient, will be loved by the Father, and will enjoy dwelling with the Father and the Son. While the fulfillment of this conditional statement (a third-class condition in Greek) is only probable, the description of the one who dwells with the Father and the Son is not merely probable but absolutely clear: he or she loves Jesus and is obedient.[11] Earlier in the chapter Jesus clarifies what is required to dwell with him in the house with many rooms (14:2): people must believe in Jesus ("Believe in God; believe also in me" [14:1b]). Thus, the one who dwells with the Father and the Son is one who believes in Jesus, who loves Jesus, and who obeys Jesus.

Third, John 15:10 states, "If you keep my commandments, you will abide in my love, just as I have kept my Father's commandments and abide in his love." Notice the equivalence of the two parts of the condition. Obedience (keeping Jesus's commands) demonstrates a continuance (abiding) in Jesus's love, i.e., salvation.

SUMMARY

Jesus does not mince words when it comes to his expectations for his followers. He asserts again and again that those who believe in him will show their belief in how they live. We have seen that he uses metaphors about fruit bearing (parable of the soils, fruit-producing trees, and the discourse about the vine and branches) and sheep (who hear his voice and follow him) as well as conditional statements of fact to assert that all true disciples of Jesus will bear fruit, keep his words, and follow him. They will persevere in good works.

We turn next to the apostle who had more to say about perseverance than any other writer in the New Testament: Paul of Tarsus.

---

11. James L. Boyer, "Third (and Fourth) Class Conditions," *GTJ* 3 (1982): 168.

CHAPTER 3

THE TEACHING OF PAUL

Paul's thirteen letters contain numerous references to believers persevering in obedience. Consider with me Paul's teaching under four headings: (1) failing to persevere reveals unbelief; (2) persevering demonstrates true belief; (3) statements of God's promises help believers persevere; and (4) indicative statements display righteous responses.

FAILING TO PERSEVERE REVEALS UNBELIEF

If failure to bear spiritual fruit shows that someone is an unbeliever, then *only* believers who are obedient will persevere and, further, *all* believers must persevere because if they do not persevere, they prove to be unbelievers. Three texts validate this truth.

- First Corinthians 15:1–2: "Now I would remind you, brothers, of the gospel I preached to you, which you received, in which you stand, and by which you are being saved, if you hold fast to the word I preached to you—unless you believed in vain." Failure to hold fast demonstrates a lack of true belief, and likewise holding fast demonstrates true belief.[1]
- Second Corinthians 13:5: "Examine yourselves, to see whether you are in the faith. Test yourselves. Or do you not realize this about yourselves, that Jesus Christ is in you?—unless indeed you fail to meet the test!" This verse assumes that verifiable evidence exists in an individual's

1. McCune, *Systematic Theology*, 3:183, states, "If the Corinthians had believed a wrong message or a distorted gospel not based on the resurrection of Christ, their faith would be false and thus unenduring."

life that demonstrates he or she is a true believer, and an inability to recognize such evidence indicates absolute failure. Contrariwise, believers will find evidence of spiritual fruit when they examine themselves, proving that they are truly saved.[2]

- Second Timothy 2:12b: "If we deny him, he also will deny us." Denial of Christ in this context means being unwilling to endure persecution for the name of Christ, and God's response of denying them points to his rejection of them and their eternal damnation.

PERSEVERING DEMONSTRATES TRUE BELIEF

Paul makes conditional statements which are the semantic opposites to those in the previous section. In these two passages, the readers' perseverance in obedient actions shows that they are true believers.

- Colossians 1:21–23: "And you, who once were alienated and hostile in mind, doing evil deeds, he has now reconciled in his body of flesh by his death, in order to present you holy and blameless and above reproach before him, if indeed you continue in the faith, stable and steadfast, not shifting from the hope of the gospel that you heard, which has been proclaimed in all creation under heaven, and of which I, Paul, became a minister." Continuance in the faith is shown by not shifting from the hope of the gospel, and this continuance demonstrates that the Colossian believers have been reconciled.[3]

---

2. Some Christians are paralyzed by a verse like 2 Cor 13:5, for they fear that they are not good enough to pass the test. But Paul does not quantify the spiritual fruit; rather, he asserts that unbelievers will not find *any* spiritual fruit in their self-examination. See the discussion of assurance in chapter 1 for more explanation.

   For those who basically seek to be perfect, Schreiner, *Run to Win the Prize*, 51–67, shows how the NT teaching about perseverance does not require perfection because the Bible calls believers to seek forgiveness when they sin (1 John 1:9), perfection occurs only at the resurrection (Phil 3:12–16), the epistles call Christians to put sin to death, Christians stumble in many ways (James 3:2), and even sinning Christians are "saved through fire" (1 Cor 3:10–17).

3. John Piper, *Providence* (Wheaton, IL: Crossway, 2020), 628–29, states that the "design of this reconciliation includes the present path of imperfect blamelessness that Paul prays for as the pathway to the perfection of [the] last day" when believers will be presented holy and blameless before God. Also, Peterson, "The Perseverance of the Saints," 96–99.

- Second Timothy 2:12a: "If we endure, we will also reign with him." Endurance in the context is a willingness to continue to believe and obey even in the midst of persecution for believing.

STATEMENTS OF GOD'S PROMISES HELP BELIEVERS PERSEVERE

Whenever Paul makes a clear pronouncement of God's promise, provision, or decision to do something for his children, we have certain evidence that God will fulfill that work. We have at least four examples of this teaching in Paul's letters.

- Romans 8:29: "For those whom he foreknew he also predestined to be conformed to the image of his Son, in order that he might be the firstborn among many brothers." Conformity to Christ's image, which God demands of the believer (Rom 12:2), is also something he predestines, and this predestining work is part of the "golden chain" of God's soteriological purpose, which includes foreknowing, predestining, calling, justifying, and glorifying.[4]
- Philippians 1:6: "And I am sure of this, that he who began a good work in you will bring it to completion at the day of Jesus Christ." While there is some debate as to what the good work in the Philippians' lives is exactly, most agree that it refers to the outworking of their salvation (Phil 2:12–13) as seen by those around them.[5] God will help the Philippians to persevere in this "good work" until Christ returns.
- First Thessalonians 5:23–24: "Now may the God of peace himself sanctify you completely, and may your whole spirit and soul and body be kept blameless at the coming of our Lord Jesus Christ. He who calls you is faithful; he will surely do it." Paul prays for the Thessalonians' *present* sanctification, and Paul is praying that it would be carried out completely. But this is more than a prayer, since Paul states that God in his faithfulness "will

4. Piper, *Providence*, 614.
5. For example, see Gordon D. Fee, *Paul's Letter to the Philippians*, NICNT (Grand Rapids: Eerdmans, 1995), 87.

surely do it." Thus, God ensures that his children will persevere in holiness and be kept blameless to the end.

- Second Thessalonians 3:3–4: "But the Lord is faithful. He will establish you and guard you against the evil one. And we have confidence in the Lord about you, that you are doing and will do the things that we command." Paul points to the Lord's faithfulness and power to guard the Thessalonians from the attacks of the evil one. Furthermore, this guarding includes protecting the Thessalonians in their obedience. Paul has confidence that they will continue to act obediently because he knows that the Lord is faithful and powerful to help them persevere in good works.

INDICATIVE STATEMENTS DISPLAY RIGHTEOUS RESPONSES

The largest number of biblical texts supporting the doctrine of perseverance in Paul are found in this fourth section of the chapter. I will organize these by letter and will proceed canonically.

Romans and Righteous Responses

I have discovered fifteen righteous responses in Romans, but I will limit our study to only seven.[6]

Rejoicing in Hope, Tribulations, and God (Rom 5:2–3, 11)

- "Through him we have also obtained access by faith into this grace in which we stand, and we rejoice in hope of the glory of God. Not only that, but we rejoice in our sufferings, knowing that suffering produces endurance" (5:2–3).
- "More than that, we also rejoice in God through our Lord Jesus Christ, through whom we have now received reconciliation" (5:11).

In 5:1–3 Paul gives two results of justification: peace with God and rejoicing. If all believers experience peace with God, they must also all experience rejoicing in both hope and tribulations. Furthermore,

6. For further explanation and exegesis of all fifteen passages, see Pratt, "The Relationship between Justification and Spiritual Fruit." The other passages not treated here are Rom 5:5; 17b; 8:4–5, 14–15, 29.

believers rejoice in God (5:11). Rejoicing (boasting) is a righteous response to the prompting of the Spirit.[7]

Walking in Newness of Life (Rom 6:4)

- "We were buried therefore with him by baptism into death, in order that, just as Christ was raised from the dead by the glory of the Father, we too might walk in newness of life."

All believers are united with Christ by baptism into his death. This is one of the metaphors Paul uses to describe the transfer all believers experience when they leave the old realm of sin "in Adam" and enter the new realm of life "in Christ." As a result of the believers' death to sin, they "walk in newness of life." This means that all believers who have been united with Christ now live ("walk") obediently. So when God, who is the unexpressed agent of the passive verb "buried," acts by uniting someone with Christ, his actions always have a certain result.[8] Therefore, all who are buried with Christ by baptism into his death will live obediently. Paul uses a similar grammatical construction in 8:4 to describe the obedient actions of all believers (they "walk . . . according to the Spirit"). Furthermore, those same believers "set their minds on the things of the Spirit" (8:5).[9]

Being Ashamed of Past Sin (Rom 6:21)

- "But what fruit were you getting at that time from the things of which you are now ashamed? For the end of those things is death."

---

7. The ESV translates the Greek word (*kauchaomai*) as "rejoice." Typically, this word means "to take pride in something, boast, glory, pride oneself, brag" (Bauer-Danker-Arndt-Gingrich). But "rejoice" is a legitimate rendering, seeking to show the positive nature of the Christian's response and perhaps minimizing any negative connotations that an English reader might attach to "boasting."
8. Grammarians refer to this use of the conjunction *hina* as showing both purpose and result. Wallace, *Greek Grammar*, 473–74. Paul uses this same conjunction to show result as he makes a similar point about perseverance in Rom 7:4 and 8:4.
9. Remember as well that the "mind set on the things of the Spirit" will not be so oriented perfectly, completely, or continuously. But that the mind is set on the things of the Spirit at all is evidence of Holy Spirit transformation (2 Cor 3:12–18).

When Paul contrasts the former lifestyles of the Roman believers (6:20–21) with their present lifestyles (6:22), he speaks of what they were like before and how they respond now. One of their present responses is an attitude of shame ("things of which you are *now* ashamed") regarding pre-conversion activities. This attitude is a righteous response of believers; indeed, all believers have left their enslavement to sin and become slaves of God (6:17–19), and all believers are ashamed of what they were and of what they did prior to entering the service of their new master.

Producing Fruit Leading to Sanctification (Rom 6:22; 7:4)

- "But now that you have been set free from sin and have become slaves of God, the fruit you get leads to sanctification and its end, eternal life" (6:22).
- "Likewise, my brothers, you also have died to the law through the body of Christ, so that you may belong to another, to him who has been raised from the dead, in order that we may bear fruit for God" (7:4).

According to 6:22, all Christians have received freedom from sin, enslavement to God, fruit leading to sanctification, and eternal life. These results are true for all believers, and one of these is clearly a righteous response—fruit leading to sanctification. Bearing fruit is also the result of all who have died to the law in their union with Christ (7:4).

Serving in Newness of the Spirit (Rom 7:6)

- "But now we are released from the law, having died to that which held us captive, so that we serve in the new way of the Spirit and not in the old way of the written code."

Two factors show that serving in newness of the Spirit is an inevitable righteous response. First, Paul uses a result infinitive clause indicating that all who have been released from the law serve in newness of the Spirit.[10] And second, Paul compares the believers'

---

10. Grammarians agree that the use of the conjunction *hōste* with the infinitive shows result. F. Blass and A. Debrunner, *A Greek Grammar of the New Testament and Other Early*

service in the Spirit with life under the old covenant ("oldness of the letter"), thus making a clear connection to the new-covenant blessing of Spirit-imprinted obedience on the heart of all new-covenant participants.

Groaning for Bodily Redemption (Rom 8:23)

- "And not only the creation, but we ourselves, who have the firstfruits of the Spirit, groan inwardly as we wait eagerly for adoption as sons, the redemption of our bodies."

We know all believers have the firstfruits of the Spirit, and all are looking forward to the redemption of their bodies.[11] This is not so much a groan of complaint as it is a groan of anticipation, a longing for future adoption and presence with the Lord (probably similar to the idea Paul expresses in Philippians 1:23 where he longs to depart and to be with Christ).[12]

Expressing Love for God (Rom 8:28)

- "And we know that for those who love God all things work together for good, for those who are called according to his purpose."

For whom does God cause all things to work together for good? (1) "Those who are called according to his purpose" and (2) "those who love God." Loving God is an inevitable and certain reality for those who have been called.

At least ten more verses in Paul's letters demonstrate that all believers have righteous responses to the ministry of the Spirit that result in their persevering obedience.

Christian Literature, trans. and rev. Robert W. Funk (Chicago: University of Chicago Press, 1961), §391; Wallace, *Greek Grammar*, 593.

11. Douglas J. Moo, *A Theology of Paul and His Letters* (Grand Rapids: Zondervan Academic, 2021), 228, explains that the firstfruits of the Spirit is "God's 'downpayment' on all he has yet to accomplish for [believers] . . . as they long for their hope to come to fruition."
12. Douglas J. Moo, *The Letter to the Romans*, 2nd ed., NICNT (Grand Rapids: Eerdmans, 2018), 542–43.

The Corinthian Letters and Righteous Responses

We examine only one text in the Corinthian letters, but please note also that 1 Corinthians 8:3, 2 Corinthians 5:16, and 2 Corinthians 9:8 provide examples of righteous responses made by all believers.

- Second Corinthians 3:18: "And we all, with unveiled face, beholding the glory of the Lord, are being transformed into the same image from one degree of glory to another. For this comes from the Lord who is the Spirit."

In 2 Corinthians 3, Paul is explaining the effects of the new-covenant ministry of the Spirit through Paul and his associates (the "us" who are the ministers of the new covenant [3:6]). He contrasts the glory of the Mosaic covenant with the greater glory of the new covenant four times in 3:7–11, and then he marvels in the blessing of the freedom from spiritual blindness that new-covenant believers enjoy as opposed to the blindness that law-following Israelites still retain (3:12–17).[13] Verse 18 is the culminating verse of the chapter, as Paul delineates three key ideas: (a) new-covenant believers behold the glory of the Lord because their faces have been unveiled, (b) new-covenant believers are being transformed, and (c) this transformation takes place by means of the ministry of the Holy Spirit.

Paul clearly equates the new-covenant blessings with the transformation of all believers, which is precisely what two key new-covenant texts promised. First, Jeremiah 32:40b states, "I will put the fear of me in their hearts, that they may not turn from me." Failing to turn away from the Lord means that new-covenant believers live obediently.[14] Second, Ezekiel 36:27 declares, "I will put my Spirit within you, and cause you to walk in my statutes and be careful to obey my rules."[15] Both of these

13. Here are the four contrasts in 2 Cor 3:7–11: "ministry of death" in v. 7 with the "ministry of the Spirit" in v. 8; the "ministry of condemnation" in v. 9a with the "ministry of righteousness" in v. 9b; "what once had glory has come to have no glory at all" in v. 10a with "the glory that surpasses it" in v. 10b; and what was "being brought to an end" in v. 11a with "what is permanent" in v. 11b.
14. Piper, *Providence*, 618, 639–40.
15. Piper, *Providence*, 625. Piper connects Ezekiel's words ("I will put my Spirit within you") with those of Jer 31:33: "I will put my law within them and I will write it on their hearts." Also see the connection to the new covenant and the heart of flesh God promises in Ezek 11:19–20 (Lorraine Boettner, *The Reformed Doctrine of Predestination* [Phillipsburg, NJ: Presbyterian & Reformed, 1963], 199).

OT texts speak to God's promise to transform new-covenant believers through the ministry of the Spirit. Doug Moo's comments provide a helpful summary of this discussion: "Central to the new covenant that God promises to 'cut' with his people in the last days is his own provision for the peoples' obedience—an obedience that was singularly lacking in the history of Israel under the Torah. A Spirit-fueled conformity to God's will is therefore a central and distinguishing characteristic of new-realm living."[16]

The Prison Epistles and Righteous Responses

- Ephesians 2:10: "For we are his workmanship, created in Christ Jesus for good works, which God prepared beforehand, that we should walk in them." Using new-creation language, Paul argues that all Christians have been saved for the purpose of doing good works that God prepared *before* Christians would "walk in them." This is language reminiscent of 1:4, where God "chose us in [Christ] before the foundation of the world," and it reminds all readers that just as certainly as the believers' election was foreordained, so also is their persevering obedience.
- Philippians 1:6: "And I am sure of this, that he who began a good work in you will bring it to completion at the day of Jesus Christ."
- Philippians 2:13: "For it is God who works in you, both to will and to work for his good pleasure." This indicative statement serves as the foundation for the imperative in 2:12 ("work out your own salvation"). Believers can obey this command because God produces the fruits of both a Spirit-driven willingness and a Spirit-motivated action in their lives.
- Colossians 1:5b–6: "Of this [hope] you have heard before in the word of the truth, the gospel, which has come to you, as indeed in the whole world it is bearing fruit and increasing—as it also does among you, since the day you heard it and understood the grace of God in truth." The gospel is bearing fruit and increasing in that the Colossians have heard and understood the grace of God. The Colossians have embraced the gospel,

16. Moo, *Theology of Paul*, 610.

and it is bearing fruit and increasing among them not only in the form of new converts but also in "the fruit of spiritual character" evidenced in the Colossians themselves.[17]

The Pastorals and Righteous Responses

- Second Timothy 4:8: "Henceforth there is laid up for me the crown of righteousness, which the Lord, the righteous judge, will award to me on that Day, and not only to me but also to all who have loved his appearing." The crown that is righteousness[18] is received by all who love Christ's appearing. Since every believer will be declared righteous at the final judgment (Rom 5:19) due to the cross work of Christ (2 Cor 5:21), every believer also loves his appearing and demonstrates this righteous response.[19]
- Titus 2:14: "Who gave himself for us to redeem us from all lawlessness and to purify for himself a people for his own possession who are zealous for good works." Here believers are described as "chosen" ("his own possession") and "zealous for good works." Since all believers are chosen, all believers are also zealous to do good works. This is an attitude or desire that cannot come from an unbelieving heart (Rom 3:10–12) but can only be generated by the work of the Spirit.

SUMMARY

In this chapter we have considered four groups of passages in Paul's writings that support the biblical doctrine of perseverance: (1) failing to persevere reveals unbelief, (2) persevering demonstrates true belief, (3) statements of God's promises help believers persevere, and (4) indicative statements display righteous responses. Paul expects all believers to be fruit bearers, to "go the distance" as they live out the calling to which they have been called.

Thus far in part 1 we have investigated the teaching of Jesus and Paul with regard to perseverance. We turn now to what the General Epistles reveal about this important doctrine.

---

17. McCune, *Systematic Theology,* 3:186.
18. This is certainly a genitive of apposition. See Wallace, *Beyond the Basics,* 95–100.
19. John Piper, *The Pleasures of God* (Portland: Multnomah, 1991), 297, concurs that this love of Christ's appearing is a necessary response of all true believers.

CHAPTER 4

THE TEACHING OF THE GENERAL EPISTLES

Having considered the New Testament teaching on perseverance in the teaching of Jesus and Paul, we now turn to the General Epistles. I have organized these verses under the same four headings used for Paul's letters: (1) failing to persevere reveals unbelief; (2) persevering demonstrates true belief; (3) statements of God's promises help believers persevere; and (4) indicative statements display righteous responses.

FAILING TO PERSEVERE REVEALS UNBELIEF

Just as we found in Paul's letters, so also several texts in the General Epistles show that unbelievers do not continue to believe and obey. Therefore, these examples show that continuance in obedience will be evidenced in the lives of true believers.

- Hebrews 12:14: "Strive for peace with everyone, and for the holiness without which no one will see the Lord." If someone does not have a holy life, he will not have the privilege of seeing the Lord in eternity. "Holiness" in this verse is speaking of progressive sanctification because it is something the believer is to strive to achieve (i.e., it is not referring to past sanctification or future sanctification but to present sanctification, without which no one will see the Lord). The implication of the command is that believers will pursue holiness since failure to live a holy life—to be obedient—will result in final damnation.
- James 2:14–17, 26: "What good is it, my brothers, if someone says he has faith but does not have works? If a brother or sister is poorly clothed and lacking in daily food, and

one of you says to them, 'Go in peace, be warmed and filled,' without giving them the things needed for the body, what good is that? So also faith by itself, if it does not have works, is dead. . . . For as the body apart from the spirit is dead, so also faith apart from works is dead." I have not included the entire text from this section of James's discussion of faith and works, but these verses show James's big point: a faith that does not show itself in good works is a dead faith. And only those who do show their faith in their good works are true believers who persevere in good works.

- First John 2:19: "They went out from us, but they were not of us; for if they had been of us, they would have continued with us. But they went out, that it might become plain that they all are not of us." Failure to continue with the apostle and his associates in the Christian faith demonstrates that they were not true believers. Thus, persevering in the faith would have been shown by a willingness to stay and to "continue" in fellowship with the apostle and the apostolic faith he promoted.
- Second John 9: "Everyone who goes on ahead and does not abide in the teaching of Christ, does not have God. Whoever abides in the teaching has both the Father and the Son." John typically uses "abide" (*menō*) to indicate continuance or remaining.[1] In this case the false believer does not continue in the teaching (as those described in 1 John 2:19), but the true believer does continue, or abide, in the teaching of Christ and does persevere in the faith.

PERSEVERING DEMONSTRATES TRUE BELIEF

The general epistles show that believers persevere and so demonstrate true belief in three ways: (a) heeding the warnings of Hebrews, (b) passing the tests of faith in the Johannine epistles, and (c) meeting conditions that Hebrews and Peter provide.

Heeding the Warnings of Hebrews

Our first group of texts that demonstrate perseverance of believers is rhetorical rather than textual in nature. By this I refer to the *function* of

1. Raymond E. Brown, *The Epistles of John*, AB (New York: Doubleday, 1982), 259–61.

warnings in the NT and in Hebrews particularly. Why does the author of Hebrews use warnings? I will answer this question by considering the purpose of the letter and the makeup of the audience. Then, based on this information, I will discuss the five warning passages and how they function with regard to perseverance.

The author's *purpose* for writing is to exhort his hearers to have faith in Jesus as the supreme and unique Son of God and faithful high priest by holding fast to Jesus and obeying his Word. He accomplishes this goal by giving exposition and warning.[2]

The main *audience* of the book is Jewish Christians in Rome with a Hellenistic background. They likely came out of synagogues in Rome when they were saved, and for this reason there are some Gentiles among them as well.[3]

There are five warning passages in Hebrews (2:1–4; 3:7–4:13; 5:11–6:12; 10:19–39; 12:14–29). Each of these passages contains four components: (1) a warning/exhortation, (2) subjects of the warning, (3) the sin committed (e.g., apostasy), and (4) the consequences of the sin.[4] While interpreters are generally agreed regarding (1) and (3), there are basically five different approaches to the answers for (2) and (4).[5]

- True believer: Loss of salvation (the standard Arminian approach)
- True believer: Loss of reward (the standard Free Grace approach)
- True believer: Hypothetical loss of salvation
- Professing but false believer: Eternal condemnation
- True believer: Conceivable consequences

---

2. Andrew H. Trotter Jr., *Interpreting the Epistle to the Hebrews*, Guides to New Testament Exegesis (Grand Rapids: Baker, 1997), 86–87.
3. See the commentaries on these issues of audience and location. There is general agreement among them in regard to the ethnic makeup of the audience as well as to the provenance of the letter. Of course, the main point, regardless of the ethnicity or location of the readers, is that they are believers. See Rodney J. Decker, "The Original Readers of Hebrews," *JMAT* 3.2 (1999): 20–49.
4. For an excellent layout of the structure and meaning of the warning passages, see Scot McKnight, "The Warning Passages of Hebrews: A Formal Analysis and Theological Conclusions," *TrinJ* 13 (1992): 21–59.
5. Three helpful resources that lay out these views include Bruce Compton, "Persevering and Falling Away: A Re-examination of Hebrews 6:4–6," *DBSJ* 1 (1996): 135–67; Herbert W. Bateman IV, ed., *Four Views on the Warning Passages in Hebrews* (Grand Rapids: Kregel Academic, 2007); and Schreiner and Caneday, *The Race Set Before Us*, 19–45. Schreiner and Caneday argue for the fifth view delineated here.

Various Reformed scholars embrace the last three views, though the fourth view is the most common Reformed interpretation.[6]

While space limitations prevent me from defending a view here, I believe the best approach is view five with a nod toward view four as well. So how does this fit with what the writer of Hebrews is trying to say in his letter and how does the writer use the warnings to accomplish his purpose?

Since his audience is primarily made up of true believers,[7] the author uses these warnings as a means of helping his readers to persevere, to hold on to Jesus. The rhetorical function of the warnings is "to appeal to the mind to conceive how actions have consequences."[8] In this way God is using the warnings to speak to both the true believers and the professing believers in the audience.[9] For the believers, the warnings serve to encourage them to "hold on" (4:14; 10:23) and to persevere in the faith to the end. For the professing, but false, believers, the warnings remind them that failing to persevere will result in eternal damnation (2:3; 4:11; 6:4–6). Thus, the warning passages of Hebrews remind us that continuing in the faith with right belief and right actions is the expectation and necessity for the true children of God.

---

6. There is a sixth view that combines views (4) and (5). It suggests that the audience was mixed, consisting of both true and false believers. C. Adrian Thomas, *A Case for Mixed-Audience with Reference to the Warning Passages in the Book of Hebrews* (New York: Peter Lang, 2008), 15–16, states, "The best way to understand these warning passages in Hebrews is to view them in the context of a mixed-community. . . . That is, the author of Hebrews writes under the assumption that his community, like any other New Testament community, is a community of professing believers in which profession must be tested. . . . Of course, not knowing for sure who these individuals are, he addresses the whole body as though all were believers, while at the same time making indirect references to elements of concern in the congregation."
7. There are two lines of support for the idea that the audience is made up of true believers: (1) the author uses first-person plural pronouns to include himself along with his readers throughout the book (3:1, 6, 14; 4:14; 6:9; 10:23; 12:4, 22); and (2) the readers had already faithfully endured persecution for their faith (10:32–34).
8. Schreiner and Caneday, *Race Set Before Us*, 207.
9. McCune, *Systematic Theology*, 3:184, states, "These warnings are concerned with professing but false believers, but since no one knows for certain where the line between the living and the dead is exactly in a group of professing Christians, the warnings are addressed to all." Buist Fanning, "A Classical Reformed View," in Bateman, *Four Views on the Warning Passages in Hebrews*, 218 (especially n99), agrees. I think, however, that the emphasis lies in the other direction. The writer of Hebrews was primarily thinking of motivating the true believers in his audience toward perseverance in good works and secondarily of warning false believers.

Passing the Tests of Faith

Our second set of texts come from the Johannine Epistles, where we find the well-known "tests of life."[10] John gives three tests so that the reader can know that he or she has eternal life (1 John 5:13).

Doctrinal Test: Do You Believe Jesus Is the Son of God?

- First John 4:1–3: "Beloved, do not believe every spirit, but test the spirits to see whether they are from God, for many false prophets have gone out into the world. By this you know the Spirit of God: every spirit that confesses that Jesus Christ has come in the flesh is from God, and every spirit that does not confess Jesus is not from God. This is the spirit of the antichrist, which you heard was coming and now is in the world already."
- First John 4:14–16: "And we have seen and testify that the Father has sent his Son to be the Savior of the world. Whoever confesses that Jesus is the Son of God, God abides in him, and he in God. So we have come to know and to believe the love that God has for us. God is love, and whoever abides in love abides in God, and God abides in him."

Moral Test: Do You Obey the Commands of God?

- First John 2:3–6: "And by this we know that we have come to know him, if we keep his commandments. Whoever says 'I know him' but does not keep his commandments is a liar, and the truth is not in him, but whoever keeps his word, in him truly the love of God is perfected. By this we may know that we are in him: whoever says he abides in him ought to walk in the same way in which he walked."
- First John 2:29: "If you know that he is righteous, you may be sure that everyone who practices righteousness has been born of him."

---

10. Robert Law, *The Tests of Life: A Study of the First Epistle of St. John* (1913; repr., Grand Rapids: Baker Academic, 1968), is typically credited as the first to use the phrase "tests of life" to describe the evidences of true belief in 1 John.

Love Test: Do You Love the People of God?

- First John 4:19–21: "We love because he first loved us. If anyone says, "I love God," and hates his brother, he is a liar; for he who does not love his brother whom he has seen cannot love God whom he has not seen. And this commandment we have from him: whoever loves God must also love his brother."
- First John 3:14: "We know that we have passed out of death into life, because we love the brothers. Whoever does not love abides in death."

For John, the believer's perseverance is demonstrated by whether or not she believes in Jesus as Son of God come in the flesh, lives obediently, and loves other Christians. Indeed, we know that someone is a Christian because they persevere in these righteous ways.

Meeting the Conditions of Hebrews and 2 Peter

The third way we see the General Epistles encouraging perseverance is in the use of conditional statements that show that the hearers are truly Christians as they fulfill the conditions.

- Hebrews 3:14: "For we have come to share in Christ, if indeed we hold our original confidence firm to the end." The perfect tense form, *gegonamen,* is significant in that the writer does not use the future tense to indicate that perseverance will result in salvation if we persevere; rather, the perfect tense "proves that we have already come to share in Christ" and that we continue to do so if we hold fast.[11] D. A. Carson makes this point regarding the perfect even more clearly: "It follows from this verse that although perseverance is mandated, it is also the evidence of what has taken place in the past. Put another way, perseverance becomes one of the essential ingredients of what it means to be a Christian, of what a partaker of Christ is and does. If persevering shows we have (already) come to share in Christ, it can only be because sharing in Christ has perseverance for

11. Piper, *Providence*, 607.

its inevitable fruit."[12] This verse is stating the same truth as 1 Corinthians 15:1–2 in that holding firm shows that one shares in Christ.

- Second Peter 1:10: "Therefore, brothers, be all the more diligent to confirm your calling and election, for if you practice these qualities [virtue, knowledge, self-control, steadfastness, godliness, brotherly affection, love] you will never fall." Possessing these fruits shows that one is a Christian and will never fall eternally.

STATEMENTS OF GOD'S PROMISES HELP BELIEVERS PERSEVERE

The General Epistles include one example of God's ability and commitment to help believers in persevering: "Now to him who is able to keep you from stumbling and to present you blameless before the presence of his glory with great joy, to the only God, our Savior, through Jesus Christ our Lord, be glory, majesty, dominion, and authority, before all time and now and forever. Amen" (Jude 24–25). Not only is God able to keep a believer from stumbling and help him to persevere in good works, but God does this because he is faithful to his promises (e.g., 1 Thess 5:24; 2 Thess 3:3) and has the power to fulfill them.

INDICATIVE STATEMENTS DISPLAY RIGHTEOUS RESPONSES

The General Epistles also provide several straightforward indicative statements that believers persevere in good works.

- Hebrews 9:13–14: "For if the blood of goats and bulls, and the sprinkling of defiled persons with the ashes of a heifer, sanctify for the purification of the flesh, how much more will the blood of the Christ, who through the eternal Spirit offered himself without blemish to God, purify our conscience from dead works to serve the living God." In an amazing act of grace, the blood of Christ accomplishes two wonderful effects: (1) it clears away the defiling effects of dead works, and (2) it puts in motion a life of obedient service for God.[13] Thus, we see that all Christians have received a purified conscience that results in obedient actions.

12. Carson, *Exegetical Fallacies*, 85. Also, Peterson, "The Perseverance of the Saints," 103–6.
13. Piper, *Providence*, 632.

- Hebrews 10:39: "But we are not of those who shrink back and are destroyed, but of those who have faith and preserve their souls." The author of Hebrews contrasts those who fail to persevere ("shrink back") with those who "have faith and preserve their souls." Two observations are in order: (1) the author includes himself and his readers as those who have faith by using the first-person plural pronoun "we"; and (2) having faith is described in the Old Testament citation from Habakkuk 2:3b–4 in the previous verse where the one who shrinks back is contrasted with the righteous one who lives by faith. Thus, the author maintains that true believers live faithfully in obedience.
- James 1:12: "Blessed is the man who remains steadfast under trial, for when he has stood the test he will receive the crown of life, which God has promised to those who love him." The crown that is life (an appositional genitive similar to 2 Timothy 4:8) is given to all believers. In this verse its recipients love God and remain steadfast under trial. Both of these righteous responses are true of Christians showing their perseverance in the faith.
- First Peter 1:1–2: "Peter, an apostle of Jesus Christ, to those who are elect exiles of the dispersion in Pontus, Galatia, Cappadocia, Asia, and Bithynia, according to the foreknowledge of God the Father, in the sanctification of the Spirit, for obedience to Jesus Christ and for sprinkling with his blood: May grace and peace be multiplied to you." Peter uses the prepositional phrase, "for obedience," to show the purpose/result of their election.[14] God's elected children have been chosen to obey.[15] Thus, Peter

14. Murray J. Harris, *Prepositions and Theology in the Greek New Testament* (Grand Rapids: Zondervan Academic, 2012), 90; Thomas R. Schreiner, *1, 2 Peter, Jude*, NAC (Nashville: Broadman & Holman, 2003), 54–55, states, "The preposition *eis* occurs three times in the subsequent verses (vv. 3–5), and in every instance the preposition designates result. In this case, however, the result also includes the idea of purpose since Peter spoke of the outworking of God's saving plan."
15. Commentators debate the nature of this obedience: does it refer to submission to the gospel in conversion (see Schreiner, *1, 2 Peter, Jude*, 55–56; and J. Ramsey Michaels, *1 Peter*, WBC [Waco, TX: Word, 1988], 11–12) or to daily obedience of believers (1 Pet 1:14), as Wayne Grudem, *1 Peter*, TNTC (Grand Rapids: Eerdmans, 1988) argues. Peter H. Davids, *The First Epistle of Peter*, NICNT (Grand Rapids: Eerdmans, 1990), 49, provides a helpful mediating position: "Conversion is more than an intellectual believing that something is true. It is repentance, a turning from a past way of life; it is faith, a commitment to Jesus as Lord that results in a way of life characterized by obedience."

describes Christians as those who live obediently as a result of their election.

- First Peter 1:8: "Though you have not seen him, you love him. Though you do not now see him, you believe in him and rejoice with joy that is inexpressible and filled with glory." All Christians love God, and this is spiritual fruit.
- First Peter 2:24–25: "He himself bore our sins in his body on the tree, that we might die to sin and live to righteousness. By his wounds you have been healed. For you were straying like sheep, but have now returned to the Shepherd and Overseer of your souls." Those who have been healed include all believers. There are two evidences of persevering action described for those who have been healed. First, believers who have died to sin live to righteousness; in other words, they respond obediently. Second, after straying like sheep, they have returned to the Shepherd. Straying is not merely a positional concept, nor is returning. When these believers return to the Shepherd and turn from their sinful actions, they are giving evidence of obedient actions.[16]
- First John 5:3–5: "For this is the love of God, that we keep his commandments. And his commandments are not burdensome. For everyone who has been born of God overcomes the world. And this is the victory that has overcome the world—our faith. Who is it that overcomes the world except the one who believes that Jesus is the Son of God?" Christians show their love for God by obeying him, and this obedient faith is connected to the fact that they are overcomers. Thus, overcoming includes keeping God's commandments.[17]

In this chapter we have considered how the General Epistles support the doctrine of perseverance by looking at four kinds of texts: (1) failing to persevere reveals unbelief; (2) persevering demonstrates true belief; (3) statements of God's promises help believers persevere; and (4) indicative statements display righteous responses. We have come

---

16. Davids, *First Epistle of Peter*, 631.
17. James E. Rosscup, "The Overcomer of the Apocalypse," *GTJ* 3 (1982): 264. Rosscup argues that every one of the overcomer passages in 1 John and Revelation include all believers as he argues against the notion that the "overcomer" is a special class of Christian.

now to see that the General Epistles, like the instruction of Jesus and Paul, teach the biblical doctrine of perseverance.

SUMMARY

In chapters 2–4 we have traveled a lengthy road through the New Testament, mining the depths of the Scripture to find the Bible's teaching about the doctrine of perseverance. The gospel record of Jesus's teaching (see ch. 2) revealed that he employed metaphors about fruit bearing and sheep as well as conditional statements of factuality to show that believers will produce spiritual fruit, will follow their Shepherd, and will continue to do so until they die.

Chapter 3, which covered Paul's teaching, was the longest of these chapters, and we discovered four basic ways that Paul emphasized perseverance: (1) texts that showed failing to persevere revealed unbelief, (2) texts that showed persevering demonstrated true belief, (3) statements of God's promises to help believers persevere, and (4) indicative statements that displayed righteous responses.

We followed the same four categories when considering the teaching of the General Epistles here in chapter 4. This included some lengthier treatments of the warnings in Hebrews and the tests of life in the Johannine epistles.

The reader will hopefully agree that the New Testament clearly affirms and emphasizes this important doctrine. But we have not yet completed part 1 of the book; for, while we have explained *what* the indicatives of the New Testament had to say about perseverance, we still need to consider *how* God has chosen to produce persevering faith in his children. And so we advance to chapter 5, where I delineate the means by which God keeps believers in doing good works.

CHAPTER 5

THE MEANS OF PERSEVERANCE

Imagine sitting next to a river watching a log drift downstream. One might ask how it could be moving since there is no human or animal pushing it along, nor is there any wind blowing. And yet the log has come from upstream, entered our field of vision, and then floated downstream all by itself. Of course, we know that the log does not propel itself down the river. Rather, the river's current—more precisely, gravity—is the means by which the log travels.

In the same way, perseverance may appear to be occurring in the believer's life all by itself. At one moment a believer struggles with uncontrolled rage when his favorite team loses a game and then at another point downstream that same believer has changed, showing little to no anger when his team tallies another defeat. Did such a transformation just happen? Not at all. In chapters 2–4 we learned that God causes such spiritual fruit to develop in the believer's life, and this truth is revealed in the indicative statements we see throughout the New Testament (what Ján Henžel calls "the divine gift of persistence in faith").[1] However, just as the current pushed the log downstream, so also God uses means to accomplish fruit bearing in the Christian, and practicing these means is the believer's responsibility as she heeds the imperatives of the New Testament.[2]

Please consider with me five ways God helps believers to do good works and so to persevere in the faith: (1) the Word of God, (2) suffering, (3) Christian fellowship in the church, (4) prayer, and (5) and attention to spiritual duties/practice of spiritual disciplines. Indeed, these are the means by which true disciples hold fast to the Word "in an honest and good heart, and bear fruit with patience" (Luke 8:15).

1. Henžel, "'And Grace Will Lead Me Home,'" 31.
2. Henžel, "'And Grace Will Lead Me Home,'" 31.

THE WORD OF GOD

There are a number of ways the Bible helps believers to persevere in the faith. We will consider four here.

Memorizing the Word

Psalm 119:11 calls believers to hide God's Word in their hearts (which assumes the need to memorize it). Memorizing Scripture affects believers' lives positively in that this keeps them from sinning.

Meditation upon the Word

Meditating upon the Word results in doing "all that is written in it" (Josh 1:8). Furthermore, Psalm 1:2–3 states that the blessed Christian is one who delights in and meditates upon the Word with the result that he prospers in all that he does. Prospering in this context is directly related to righteous living as opposed to the behavior of the wicked.

Obeying the Word's Commands

God gives believers an abundance of both negative and positive commands or imperatives that, when obeyed, result in bearing righteous fruit. Perhaps it will help the reader to consider why God would be so gracious in giving his children divine imperatives. There are at least four. The first is rather obvious: all are born sinners, and no one loses the ability to sin until glory (Rom 3:23; 1 John 1:8–10). Second, conformation into the image of Christ (Rom 8:29; Gal 4:19) continues to take place in the believer's life, and this assumes the ongoing presence of sin as believers are transformed "from one degree of glory to another" (2 Cor 3:18). Third, believers need direction to improve and grow in their submission to the Spirit's work of sanctification because Christians are still ignorant and forgetful. Paul makes this point succinctly: "If anyone imagines that he knows something, he does not yet know as he ought to know" (1 Cor 8:2). Fourth, we need encouragement and motivation to fight sin and to resist temptation. The Puritans referred to this activity as mortification, and sadly, teaching about this important element of the Christian's experience has fallen on hard times in the present day.[3]

---

3. Sinclair B. Ferguson, *The Christian Life: A Doctrinal Introduction* (Carlisle: Banner of Truth, 1981), 147. Ferguson expands upon the meaning of mortification by providing

Heeding the Conditional Promises and Warnings of the Word

God uses the conditional promises and warnings of the Word to help Christians persevere.[4] Revelation 21:6–7 is one such promise: "And he said to me, 'It is done! I am the Alpha and the Omega, the beginning and the end. To the thirsty I will give from the spring of the water of life without payment. The one who conquers will have this heritage, and I will be his God and he will be my son.'" The promise of eternal life (expressed as receiving the water of life and being a son of God) is conditioned upon the persevering actions of thirsting and overcoming. Knowledge of this promise provides strong encouragement for believers to bear fruit.[5] Conditional warnings function in the same way: as believers consider the consequences that will come to them if they fail to heed the biblical warnings, they are motivated to obey God's Word. Notice the conditional warning of Revelation 22:18–19: "I warn everyone who hears the words of the prophecy of this book: if anyone adds to them, God will add to him the plagues described in this book, and if anyone takes away from the words of the book of this prophecy, God will take away his share in the tree of life and in the holy city, which are described in this book."

SUFFERING

God uses suffering or discipline to produce spiritual fruit in his children. Notice how the author of Hebrews explains: "For [our earthly fathers] disciplined us for a short time as it seemed best to them, but [God] disciplines us for our good, that we may share his holiness. For the moment all discipline seems painful rather than pleasant, but later it yields the peaceful fruit of righteousness to those who have been trained by it" (Heb 12:10–11). Jesus asserted that believers who are living members of the vine receive pruning (i.e., suffering) in order that they may bear more fruit (John 15:1–2). We find an illustration of this reality when Paul was called to suffer with a

five practical steps believers should follow: (1) recognize sin for what it is; (2) bring your sin into the light of God's presence; (3) recall the shame of past sin; (4) remember you are united to Christ; and (5) prayerfully seek the fruit of the Spirit (153–55).

4. Schreiner and Caneday, *The Race Set Before Us*, 41–45, provide an excellent discussion of conditional promises and warnings.
5. Ferguson, *Christian Life*, 167, reminds us that when Christians embrace God's "precious and very great promises" (2 Pet 1:4), they are encouraged and assured as they "battle on for Christ."

"thorn in the flesh." Even when God chose not to remove this thorn he responded, "Therefore, I will boast all the more gladly of my weaknesses, so that the power of Christ may rest upon me. For the sake of Christ, then, I am content with weaknesses, insults, hardships, persecutions, and calamities. For when I am weak, then I am strong" (2 Cor 12:9b–10). Boasting in weakness and being content with painful difficulties are precisely the kind of fruit described by Hebrews 12:11 and John 15:1–2.

CHRISTIAN FELLOWSHIP IN THE CHURCH

God uses the Christian fellowship of the local church to encourage believers to persevere in the faith. Hebrews makes this abundantly clear: "And let us consider how to stir up one another to love and good works, not neglecting to meet together, as is the habit of some, but encouraging one another, and all the more as you see the Day drawing near" (Heb 10:24–25). This passage encourages believers to produce the spiritual fruit of love and good works by attending the public gatherings of the church.

Paul makes this same point in at least three passages. First, many of the commands in Romans 12:3–21 relate to the relationships believers have with the other members of the body of Christ. By virtue of being members of local churches, believers have a place to use their spiritual gifts to serve one another (vv. 6–8), love and show honor to one another (v. 10), contribute to the needs of others and show hospitality to others (v. 13), rejoice and weep with others (v. 15), and live in harmony and peaceably with others (vv. 16, 18). Indeed, the kind of spiritual fruit mentioned in this passage can only occur when believers have personal relationships with other members of their local church. Second, Ephesians 4:4–16 speaks of the work wrought by the pastor-teachers of the church. They equip the saints to do the work of ministry and to build up the body so that their obedient response to this equipping results in unity, spiritual maturity, rejection of false teaching, and edifying love and speech. Again, this kind of spiritual fruit is produced by connection to an assembly where pastor-teachers are equipping. Third, Paul gives an expanded treatment of the use of spiritual gifts in the body of Christ, showing that the gifts are given for one primary reason—to build up the church body (1 Cor 14:5, 12). We see that there is a notable connection between church gathering and perseverance in good works (e.g., exercise of spiritual gifts) by the individuals in the gathered church.[6]

One of God's intended purposes for his church is for it to serve as a place where believers are encouraged to persevere and can demonstrate spiritual fruit as they serve other Christians. This is why the church is one of the vital means God uses to help believers persevere in faith and good works.

PRAYER

An underappreciated means of perseverance is prayer. Throughout the NT we see examples of prayers for others and oneself for God to bring about persevering fruit.

Prayer for Others

We begin with Jesus, whose prayers on the evening before his crucifixion illustrate how to pray for perseverance. When Jesus was still in the upper room with his disciples he prophesied that Peter would deny him three times (Luke 22:34), but even in light of that knowledge he said, "I have prayed for you that your faith may not fail" (22:32). A short time later, after Jesus and his disciples had crossed over the Kidron Valley and had entered the garden of Gethsemane, Jesus prayed, "And I am no longer in the world, but [my disciples] are in the world, and I am coming to you. Holy Father, keep them in your name, which you have given me, that they may be one, even as we are one" (John 17:11). Not only is Jesus praying for their preservation in the faith, but also for obedient fruit in their lives that would result in unifying behavior, that is, sanctifying fruit (17:17, 19).

We also see several examples of prayers for believers' perseverance in Paul's letters. For example, Philippians 1:9–11 states, "And it is my prayer that your love may abound more and more, with knowledge and all discernment, so that you may approve what is excellent, and so be pure and blameless for the day of Christ, filled with the fruit of righteousness that comes through Jesus Christ, to the glory and praise of God." Paul prays for the Colossian believers: "And so, from the day we heard, we have not ceased to pray for you, asking that you may be filled with

6. Ferguson, *Christian Life*, 168, states: "Our spiritual progress depends in measure on our being able to minister to others, and our receiving ministry from others. We are members of a body, says Paul—and the body moves, lives and grows together."

the knowledge of his will in all spiritual wisdom and understanding, so as to walk in a manner worthy of the Lord, fully pleasing to him, bearing fruit in every good work and increasing in the knowledge of God" (Col 1:9–10). The Thessalonian epistles include four prayers for perseverance: (1) "Now may our God and Father himself, and our Lord Jesus, direct our way to you, and may the Lord make you increase and abound in love for one another and for all, as we do for you, so that he may establish your hearts blameless in holiness before our God and father, at the coming of our Lord Jesus with all his saints" (1 Thess 3:11–13); (2) "Now may the God of peace himself sanctify you completely, and may your whole spirit and soul and body be kept blameless at the coming of our Lord Jesus Christ" (1 Thess 5:23); (3) "Now may our Lord Jesus Christ himself, and God our Father, who loved us and gave us eternal comfort and good hope through grace, comfort your hearts and establish them in every good work and word" (2 Thess 2:16–17); and (4) "May the Lord direct your hearts to the love of God and to the steadfastness of Christ" (2 Thess 3:5). As Paul prayed for the spiritual advancement of believers in all of these prayers, he was praying for persevering faith.

Finally, the author of Hebrews prayed for perseverance in the final benediction of his letter: "Now may the God of peace who brought again from the dead our Lord Jesus, the great shepherd of the sheep, by the blood of the eternal covenant, equip you with everything good that you may do his will, working in us that which is pleasing in his sight, through Jesus Christ, to whom be glory forever and ever. Amen" (Heb 13:20–21).

These passages are sufficient to show that praying for other believers' perseverance in the faith is exemplified by Christ and other NT authors and that prayer is a means God uses in helping Christians to bear fruit to the end of their earthly lives.

Prayer for Oneself

There is one passage that directly calls believers to pray for their own perseverance. Jude writes, "But you, beloved, building yourselves up in your most holy faith and praying in the Holy Spirit; keep yourselves in the love of God, waiting for the mercy of our Lord Jesus Christ that leads to eternal life" (Jude 20–21). While the English translation of these verses appears to give three commands and one participial clause, Jude has only one imperative ("keep yourselves in the love of God") surrounded by three subordinate participial clauses: (a) "building yourselves up in the most holy faith"; (b) "praying in the Holy Spirit"; and (c) "waiting for the mercy of our Lord Jesus Christ." While there is some debate as to how these three clauses relate to the main verb, I suggest that they all provide the means by which believers keep themselves in the love of God.[7] They do this by building themselves up, praying, and waiting so that their prayers help to keep them in the love of God, that is, to persevere in the faith.

Attention to Spiritual Duties / Practice of Spiritual Disciplines

Thus far we have considered four means by which believers persevere in the faith: (1) the Word of God, (2) suffering, (3) Christian fellowship in the church, and (4) prayer. We come now to the fifth means—attention to spiritual duties or the practice of spiritual disciplines.

Sinclair Ferguson rightly assesses the value of obedience to spiritual duties when he states, "When we go 'off the rails' spiritually, the rails we leave are those of our duties."[8] Using the biblical examples of Adam and Eve in Genesis 3 and David in 2 Samuel 11–12, Ferguson reminds us that the disregard of the basic instructions of God in season and out of season will result in spiritual failure.[9] So, one of the ways Christians persevere is by practicing spiritual disciplines.

Before proceeding with more explanation about the spiritual duties, I must clarify the distinction between this category (regarding duties) and the categories already discussed (the Word of God and prayer). This distinction is necessary because Bible intake and prayer are two duties included in any list of spiritual disciplines one might consult.[10] But when we discussed the Word and prayer as means of perseverance, we were not looking at God's calls to the Christian duties of Bible intake and prayer (i.e., the *what* of the spiritual disciplines); rather, we were examining *how* God uses the Bible and prayer to help the Christian persevere.

---

7. Schreiner, *1, 2 Peter, Jude*, 481, concurs.
8. Ferguson, *Christian Life*, 167.
9. Ferguson, *Christian Life*, 167–68.
10. I highly recommend three authors who have written on this subject: Jerry Bridges, *The Pursuit of Holiness* (Colorado Springs: NavPress, 2016) and *The Discipline of Grace: God's Role and Our Role in the Pursuit of Holiness* (Colorado Springs: NavPress, 2006); Donald S. Whitney, *Spiritual Disciplines for the Christian Life*, rev. ed. (Colorado Springs: NavPress, 2014); and David Mathis, *Habits of Grace: Enjoying Jesus through the Spiritual Disciplines* (Wheaton, IL: Crossway, 2016).

It is in the discipline of doing the duties that we are helped to persevere (they are the rails) rather than in the use of any of the particular duties. So for this fifth means the emphasis is not in the particular *use* of the duties (e.g., there are a number of duties that do not in themselves serve as means for perseverance, such as witnessing, giving, worship, fasting, or journaling); rather, the emphasis is on the *doing* of the duties—simply obeying and practicing the various spiritual disciplines that serve as means God uses to help us bear fruit to the end of our earthly lives.

God has given several duties to Christians, whether by command or example, that, if obeyed, serve as a means of helping believers to bear spiritual fruit and so to persevere in the faith. These include Bible intake, prayer, worship, evangelism, serving, giving, fasting, journaling, learning, silence and solitude,[11] mortification,[12] church membership,[13] participation in church ordinances,[14] and time management.[15] As the Christian seeks to be obedient to the practice of these spiritual disciplines, he or she is kept from falling into disqualifying sin while at the same time helped to bear fruit unto sanctification (Rom 6:22).

SUMMARY

We have now arrived at the final stop of our scriptural route in part 1, during which we have traced the NT teaching about perseverance. In chapters 2–4 we considered the indicatives of perseverance by noting the teaching of Jesus, the many statements from Paul's letters, and the corroborating declarations in the General Epistles. This chapter has provided the means of perseverance: (1) the Word of God, (2) suffering, (3) Christian fellowship in the church, (4) prayer, and (5) attention to duties.

With the scriptural foundation now established, we are ready to switch to a new track in part 2 as we become acquainted with the erroneous distortion of perseverance, particularly the threat of antinomianism in the American evangelical church.

11. Whitney, *Spiritual Disciplines*, includes all of these along with a few more. Also see Bridges, *Pursuit of Holiness*, 98–137; idem, *Discipline of Grace*; and Mathis, *Habits*.
12. Bridges, *Discipline of Grace*, 181–200.
13. Mathis, *Habits*, 145–50, shows that it is not only the practice of Christian fellowship that is important as a spiritual discipline but is even more so the believer's commitment to a local church in formal and covenantal membership.
14. Mathis, *Habits*, 173–83, provides a helpful discussion of the value of the ordinances as spiritual disciplines.
15. Mathis, *Habits*, 211–18.

PART 2

ERRONEOUS DISTORTION

CHAPTER 6

A HISTORY OF ANTINOMIANISM FROM 1600–1950

The four chapters that comprise part 2 are primarily historical rather than theological in nature as we consider one of the erroneous distortions of the doctrine of perseverance—antinomianism.[1] We will pursue this historical study in four chapters. First, chapter 6 provides a history of this teaching from the Reformation to the middle of the twentieth century. Then, chapters 7–9 investigates three current-day forms of antinomian teaching in the American evangelical church: Free Grace (chapter 7), Radical Grace (chapter 8), and Hyper-Grace (chapter 9). My hope is that in learning of these modern distortions of perseverance, believers will be able to avoid their influence and be persuaded to pursue holiness (perseverance), without which no one will see the Lord (Heb 12:14).

INTRODUCTION

Ask any daredevil on a tightrope, any gymnast on a balance beam, or any surfer on a wave, and each will affirm that balance is essential. One misstep, and injury—or even death—might occur. The same need for balance holds true in the realm of theology. Notice three examples: (1) in Christology, imbalance regarding the hypostatic union could result in the heresy of Arianism (denying the full deity of Christ) on one side or Docetism (denying the humanity of Christ) on the other; (2) regarding divine sovereignty, an overemphasis on God's control of his universe would result in

1. Other distortions of perseverance would include legalism, moralism, prosperity gospel teaching, and quietism. But I believe that the most significant distortion of perseverance, both historically and theologically, is antinomianism, as our study demonstrates.

fatalism, while a deemphasis on God's control would result in deism; and (3) when considering progressive sanctification, a disproportionate stress on God's role (evidenced in the indicatives of Scripture) might result in quietism or antinomianism just as an imbalanced emphasis on man's role (evidenced in the imperatives of Scripture) might result in legalism or moralism.

In this chapter I want to consider the last of these three examples; particularly, the problem of antinomianism in the progressive sanctification of the believer. Orthodox theologians consider antinomianism to be a clear example of a doctrinal aberration—a heresy at worst and a mistake at best—that has been the source of confusion and division among evangelical Christians for centuries. As with most theological errors, discussing antinomianism is no small task, for antinomianism has no foremost theologian, no systematic theology, no denomination or even a single church, and therefore, no set of organized beliefs.[2]

A second reason the study of antinomianism proves challenging is the reticence of its proponents to accept the nomenclature.[3] After all, who wants to identify oneself as a heretic?[4] Usually the term is applied to supposed antinomians by others, and these "hostile appellations in the context of theological debate are sometimes misplaced."[5] Key examples of this kind of treatment include Martin Luther, John Cotton, and Thomas Boston, who were each wrongly accused of being antinomians.[6] At the same time, proponents of antinomian doctrine

2. Gertrude Huehns, *Antinomianism in English History with Special Reference to the Period 1640–1660* (London: Cresset Press, 1951), 85, writes: "There never really existed an organized antinomian church."

3. William Young, "Antinomianism," in *The Encyclopedia of Christianity (Volume 1: A–Bible)* ed. Edwin Palmer, 4 vols. (Wilmington, DE: The National Foundation for Christian Education, 1964), 1:270, states, "Almost invariably, those charged with this heresy repudiate or at least reformulate the positions they are alleged to have asserted."

4. Apparently, some did not mind the epithet! For example, Washington Wilkes, *A Fearless Defence of the Leading Doctrines Preached and Received by Modern Antinomians* (London, 1830), cited in Robert W. Oliver, *History of the English Calvinistic Baptists 1771–1892 from John Gill to C. H. Spurgeon* (Carlisle, PA: Banner of Truth, 2006), 302. Also see John Warburton, *Mercies of a Covenant God* (London: Gadsby, 1878), 23, 25.

5. Mark Jones, *Antinomianism: Reformed Theology's Unwelcome Guest?* (Phillipsburg, NJ: P&R Publishing, 2013), 16.

6. The sources listed here include descriptions of the antinomian accusations made against these men and the refutation of those charges. For Luther: Young, "Antinomianism," 1:275; and Timothy J. Wengert, "Antinomianism," in *The Oxford Encyclopedia of the Reformation*, ed. Hans Hillerbrand, 4 vols. (New York: Oxford University Press, 1996), 1:51–53. For Cotton: Iain H. Murray, "Antinomianism: New England's First Controversy,"

have actually existed throughout church history, and the wise student will seek to learn how to distinguish between the false and true antinomians. But this effort to classify antinomians is fraught with difficulty because one should not approach this study with an either/or mentality. Rather, antinomianism ought to be viewed as existing on a continuum with one pole representing true antinomians (like Anne Hutchinson, about whom no one questions her lawless proclivities)[7] and the opposite pole representing false antinomians (like John Cotton, who voiced some antinomian statements but on further investigation was found to oppose antinomianism).[8]

Despite these reasons for exercising caution in this enterprise, a study of the history of antinomianism in the church, particularly from 1600–1950, proves fruitful. First, we give a simple description of antinomianism. Second, we consider the early history of antinomianism from 100–1600. Third, we study the various ways antinomianism has been manifested in England and in the American colonies (and later the United States) from 1600–1950.[9] And finally, we summarize the main tenets of antinomian teaching based on the historical study.

THE DESCRIPTION OF ANTINOMIANISM

Before describing the origins and history of antinomianism we must consider what this slippery term actually means, for its simple etymological rendering, "against law," is far from helpful.

Simple Definition of Antinomianism

To begin, let us consider three definitions, given in no particular order of significance: (1) "a tendency to exalt the transformative power of free grace on believers and to denigrate, or even deny, the role and use of

---

Banner of Truth 179–180 (1978): 30–68. For Boston: Sinclair Ferguson, *The Whole Christ: Legalism, Antinomianism, and Gospel Assurance—Why the Marrow Controversy Still Matters* (Wheaton, IL: Crossway, 2016), 77–122, 137–75.

7. See the historical section below for further discussion of Hutchinson's antinomian beliefs.
8. See Murray, "Antinomianism," 30–68, for more insights into Cotton's beliefs.
9. From the outset I face a quandary with regard to my chosen method. Should I investigate the history of antinomianism followed by the delineation of its tenets that arises from that historical study—an inductive approach? Or should I provide a definition up front so that we know which individuals and movements we should be studying as we consider the 1600–1950 time period—a deductive approach? I have chosen a hybrid arrangement by limiting my historical study with a simple set of defined criteria and then giving a full-orbed description following the historical study. I hope this proves to be fruitful.

the Moral law as revealed in the Old Testament in the lives of converted Christians;"[10] (2) "'Practical antinomianism' is the practice of lawlessness, whereas 'doctrinal antinomianism' is . . . the theological system in which good works are radically excluded;"[11] and (3) "Believers, who emphasize the unconditional promises that God makes when covenanting with His people, but then downplay what God expects of His people, tend toward an antinomistic faith."[12] Sinclair Ferguson summarizes these definitions well: "The simplest way to think of antinomianism is that it denies the role of the law in the Christian life."[13] But much more nuance is needed, and I will provide this nuance with an expanded description of antinomianism following our historical survey.

Criteria for Identifying Antinomianism

As authors delineate various antinomian errors, the student is confronted with a multitude of listings, ranging from a minimal tally of two to a gargantuan catalog of eighty-two![14] In the interest of clarity and conciseness, I will limit our historical study to two simple criteria: (1) those who are called antinomians by contemporaries and (2) those who call themselves antinomians.[15]

Given these two criteria, it is good to note two nuances in our investigation of antinomianism. First, the tendency among many antinomian writers is to state "things as either-or, when, in fact, the doctrine in question is more both-and."[16] This points to a reality that theologians

10. David Como, "Antinomianism," in *Puritans and Puritanism in Europe and America: A Comprehensive Encyclopedia*, ed. Francis J. Bremer and Tom Webster (Santa Barbara, CA: ABC-CLIO, 2006), 305.
11. Gert van den Brink, "Calvin, Witsius (1636–1708), and the English Antinomians," *Church History and Religious Culture* 91.1–2 (2011): 230.
12. Robert W. Wall, "Antinomianism," in *Anchor Bible Dictionary*, ed. David Noel Freedman, 6 vols. (New York: Doubleday, 1992), 1:263.
13. Ferguson, *Whole Christ*, 140.
14. Como, "Antinomianism," 306, has only two, while John Winthrop, *A Short Story of the Rise, Reign, and Ruin of the Antinomians, Familists, and Libertines of New England* (London: printed for Tho. Parkhurst at the Bible and Three Crowns at the lower end of Cheapside near Mercer's Chapel, 1692), 1–19, provides eighty-two errors along with eighty-two confutations. Winthrop's list is from the "front lines" in the sense that he is writing a description of the first antinomian controversy that arose in the American colonies during the 1630s.
15. We will learn of several who were called antinomians by their opponents but were later exonerated either because they changed their minds or because they were wrongly accused.
16. Jones, *Antinomianism*, 91.

often face when defending their particular viewpoint. Mark Jones and Patrick Ramsey observe, "The seventeenth century reveals that both antinomians and neonomians were typically reactionary theologians. Their reactions to the perceived excesses of certain groups were not always helpful or clearly articulated."[17] Second, "antinomians are in more serious error in what they fail to say than in what they do say."[18] This tendency to avoid providing balance and nuance to the antinomian's doctrinal hobby horses typically shows the importance of the hobby horse and the non-importance of the inarticulate element of the discussion (e.g., moral law) to the antinomian author. In this way antinomians reveal their true beliefs, emphasizing the major elements of their position and ignoring the rudiments of the doctrines with which they disagree.

THE SPARKS OF ANTINOMIANISM

Having discussed the simple definition and criteria for identifying antinomianism, we are now in a position to consider the early outbreaks of antinomianism in the history of the church from the time of its beginning through the Reformation period (100–1600).[19] The individuals and movements mentioned here are merely precursors to the more developed antinomianism considered in our next section. Nonetheless, the seeds of antinomian teaching noted here are scattered throughout Christendom both chronologically and geographically, and they would bear fruit in the centuries following the Reformation.

Pre-Reformation Period

William Young helpfully summarizes the history of antinomian teaching during these years under four headings: (1) apostolic period, (2) patristic period, (3) medieval period, and (4) mystical movements.[20]

17. Mark Jones and D. Patrick Ramsey, "The Antinomian-Neonomian Controversy in Nonconforming England (c. 1690)," in *A New Divinity: Transatlantic Reformed Evangelical Debates during the Long Eighteenth Century*, ed. Mark Jones and Michael A. G. Haykin, Reformed Historical Theology 49 (Göttingen: Vandenhoeck & Ruprecht, 2018), 23. The term "neonomian" was coined by Isaac Chauncy (1632–1712) to describe pastors who emphasized the imperatives too much (22). Perhaps a modern-day equivalent might be "legalist" or "moralist."
18. Jones, *Antinomianism*, 117.
19. While our study will not focus on examples of antinomianism in the Bible, see Wall, "Antinomianism," 1:263, for a thorough biblical survey, and Jones, *Antinomianism*, 1–3.
20. Young, "Antinomianism," 273–74.

During the *apostolic period* church fathers like Irenaeus, Clement of Alexandria, and Justin Martyr commented on the lawless teachings of the Nicolaitans and Simon Magus.[21] In the *patristic period* groups like the Adamites, Cainites, Gnostics, and Ophites arose, sharing a spirit of indifference toward the law.[22] Followers of heretical teachers like Carpocrates, Epiphanes, Cerdo, and Marcion followed similar antinomian paths.[23]

The *medieval period* produced the pantheistic teaching of Amaury of Paris and the Brethren of the Free Spirit (ca. 1200), which emphasized the importance of the Spirit apart from the rule of the law in the Christian's life.[24] Finally, *mystical writings* such as the *Theologia Germanica* (an anonymous meditation), the musings of German mystic Sebastian Franck, and the works of Hendrick Nicholas (ca. 1502–1580), whose followers were known as the Family of Love or Familists, all played a significant role in the flourishing of seventeenth-century antinomianism in England and the American colonies.[25] These Familists fell under the frequent condemnation of the Puritans due to their denial of imputed righteousness, exclusive concern with inner experience, rejection of the necessity of holy living, and belief in the present perfection of the believer.[26]

The Reformation Period

Both Calvin and Luther fought antinomian fires, but Luther's disputations against the antinomian teaching of Johann Agricola (1492–1566) are more well-known, so we begin with Luther.

Antinomianism and Martin Luther

Martin Luther famously preached a message of grace, placing a strong emphasis on the contrast between law and gospel in the justification of the sinner. For him the law had no effect on the justification of the sinner

21. Young, "Antinomianism," 273.
22. Gabriel Fackre, "Antinomianism," in The *Westminster Dictionary of Christian Theology*, ed. Alan Richardson and John Bowden (Philadelphia: Westminster Press, 1983), 27; Young, "Antinomianism," 273.
23. Young, "Antinomianism," 273–74.
24. Young, "Antinomianism," 274; Fackre, "Antinomianism," 27.
25. Como, "Antinomianism," 306; Young, "Antinomianism," 274.
26. Murray, "Antinomianism," 13; Young, "Antinomianism," 275.

because it makes demands that the sinner must obey.[27] The gospel, on the other hand, forbids doing of any sort: for "men so oppressed, terrified, miserable, anxious, and afflicted [by the guilt-driven message of the Pope] there was no need to inculcate the Law . . . [rather, they should] take refuge in the grace and mercy offered in Christ."[28]

Luther's friend, Johann Agricola (1494–1566), picked up on Luther's distinction between law and gospel and strongly objected to the preaching of the law, believing that only the preaching of the gospel was needed.[29] This reality was true for Agricola not only in preaching for justification but also in preaching for sanctification. Thus, "the gospel takes over the sin-disclosing function of the law and becomes the principle of the Christian life in penitence" with the implication that the law has no function for the believer's sanctification.[30]

In 1537, the publication of a series of anonymous theses accusing Luther and Melanchthon of legalism brought this antinomian teaching into the open as Luther argued against each accusation in a published response.[31] Luther also debated the theses in a series of three disputations occurring in 1537–1538, and finally in a formal treatise, *Against the Antinomians*, written in 1539.[32] Luther's argument with Agricola and his antinomian sympathizers would continue until Luther's death in 1546 as Luther maintained his defense of the third use of the law—"to show the believer what God requires of him."[33]

27. Van den Brink, "Calvin, Witsius, and English Antinomians," 232; J. Wayne Baker, "Sola Fide, Sola Gratia: The Battle for Luther in Seventeenth-Century England," *The Sixteenth Century Journal* 16.1 (1985): 117.
28. Martin Luther as translated and quoted in James MacKinnon, *Luther and the Reformation* (London: Longmans, Green, 1930), 4:171.
29. Baker, "Sola Fide," 116; van den Brink, "Calvin, Witsius, and English Antinomians," 230.
30. Steffen Kjeldgaard-Pedersen, "Antinomian Controversies," in *Encyclopedia of Christianity*, ed. Erwin Fuhlbusch et al., trans. Geoffrey Bromiley (Grand Rapids: Eerdmans, 1999), 1: 80.
31. Wengert, "Antinomianism," 52, summarizes the teaching of the anonymous theses: "The law belonged in the courthouse, not God's house." MacKinnon, *Luther and the Reformation*, 162–69, gives a detailed description of the theses and Luther's response. Luther was quite convinced that Agricola had been the author of said theses, though Agricola denied that he had written them (166). Agricola, however, did not deny that he affirmed everything the theses asserted regarding the condemnation of the preaching of the law to bring about repentance.
32. Martin Luther, "Against the Antinomians," in *Luther's Works*, ed. Franklin Sherman and Helmut T. Lehmann, trans. Martin H. Bertram, 55 vols. (Philadelphia: Fortress Press, 1971), 47:107–19. Baker, "Sola Fide," 117; Wengert, "Antinomianism," 52; Kjeldgaard-Pedersen, "Antinomian Controversies," 80.
33. MacKinnon, *Luther and the Reformation*, 169. MacKinnon's concluding remarks about the controversy bear repeating: "It is difficult to form a confident judgment on the merits

On a final note regarding this controversy, most would agree that Luther had modified his teaching about the law and the Christian life in his later years, whereas his early preaching spoke of the law-gospel distinction in much starker terms. Agricola merely followed Luther's early gospel preaching while Luther settled upon the need to emphasize the law because of the "softly singing Antinomians" who "make men secure who are of themselves already so secure that they fall away from grace."[34]

Following Luther's death, two more rounds of antinomian controversies play out in the sixteenth century. First, Lutherans attempted to reconcile Luther's theology to Melanchthon's, who viewed the gospel as including a message of repentance, a position quite similar to Agricola's.[35] Second, disputes regarding the support or rejection of the third use of the law (advocated by both Luther and Melanchthon) resulted in an attempt to incorporate these conflicting positions in Article 6 of the Formula of Concord (1580), which emphasized "the necessity of good works and the third use of the law alongside the spontaneity of good works and the law's singularly coercive powers."[36]

Antinomianism and John Calvin

Though its occurrence is lesser known, John Calvin sparred with an antinomian group known as the Libertines.[37] This group espoused a spiritualistic pantheism, denied human agency and accountability,

---

of the controversy. It was to a certain extent, conditioned by the personal character of the disputants." He assesses Luther as being too touchy about having his authority questioned, and he believes Agricola possessed unworthy motives and underhanded tactics (176). Also see Young, "Antinomianism," 275, for a summary of the erroneous theses taught by the antinomians: (1) men are not to be prepared for the gospel or conversion by the preaching of the law; (2) repentance is not to be taught out of the Decalogue or any law of Moses but from the violation of the Son of God in the gospel; (3) when people are in the midst of sin, they only need to believe; (4) the law is not worthy to be called the Word of God; (5) a believer is above all law and all obedience; (6) good works profit nothing in salvation; and (7) our faith and NT teaching about salvation were unknown to Moses.

34. MacKinnon, *Luther and the Reformation*, 172; Baker, "Sola Fide," 117, states, "Luther himself admitted that in the early period he had emphasized the gospel almost exclusively" because in those earlier days men were terrified by their inability to keep the law in order to be saved. But by the 1530s, the needs of the audience had changed since people had become secure in their sinfulness. But "Luther asserted that he had not altered his teaching but simply had changed his emphasis in response to a different situation."
35. Kjeldgaard-Pedersen, "Antinomianism," 81; Wengert, "Antinomianism," 52–53.
36. Wengert, "Antinomianism," 53.
37. Van den Brink, "Calvin, Witsius, and the English Antinomians," 230.

extended Christian liberty to all things, and excused the sins of the regenerate on the grounds that it is not the regenerate nature that sins but rather the flesh.[38] Calvin responded with a book published in Latin (1544) and French (1545) entitled *Instruction against the Fantastic and Furious Sect of Libertines who Call Themselves Spiritual.*[39] Calvin's efforts helped to stem the tide of Libertine doctrine which had infected Holland and its adjacent provinces.[40]

ANTINOMIAN FIRES IN THE CHURCH FROM 1600 TO 1950

The sparks of antinomian fervor generated during the sixteenth century stoked several fires in the ensuing centuries. Our study will seek to cover the major blazes of this time period by considering the proponents of antinomianism, their teachings, and their opponents during each of these fiery instances.

Seventeenth Century

In the previous section we considered some of the antinomian teaching that Calvin and Luther addressed. Students of the Reformation might wish that their heroes succeeded in putting such anti-law doctrine to rest, but sadly, the putrid smoke of those antinomian fires blew from central Europe and found happy homes in England and the American colonies. Historians trace three significant outbreaks of antinomianism in the seventeenth century.

Antinomianism in Puritan England

The strong emphasis on Puritan piety and practice, the rising Arminian movement within Protestantism, and the perfectionistic teaching of the Familists all contributed to the first wave of seventeenth-century antinomianism in England.[41] Influenced by the writings and preaching of such leaders as John Eaton (1574/5–1630/31), Tobias Crisp (1600–1643), John Saltmarsh (d. 1647), John Traske (1585–1636), Roger Brierley (1586–1637), and Robert Towne (1592/3–1664),

38. Young, "Antinomianism," 275–76.
39. Young, "Antinomianism," 275; van den Brink, "Calvin, Witsius, and the English Antinomians," 230. My translation based on a combination of both the Latin and French titles.
40. Young, "Antinomianism," 276, states that this was the assessment of Beza in his *Life of Calvin.*
41. Jones, *Antinomianism*, 6; and Murray, "Antinomianism," 13.

English antinomians believed themselves to be "the true defenders of free grace."[42]

Although these believers were not monolithic in their theological positions, they do appear to agree regarding some general antinomian ideas.[43] First, the moral law has no role in the lives of believers.[44] Second, believers are passive in sanctification, and any emphasis on duties in the Christian life earns the label "legalist."[45] Third, the truth of the absence of works in justification is likewise stressed in regard to sanctification; i.e., they blur justification and sanctification.[46] John Eaton's statement illustrates this confusion:

> By the power of his imputation, [God] doth so truly clothe us both within and without with this his Son's doing and fulfilling of the law perfectly, that we also continue in all things to do them in the sight of God, not inherently and actively, by our own doing, but because his Son's perfect doing all things is objectively and passively so truly *in us*, that we are made perfectly holy and righteous in the sight of God with that doing freely, and so the rigour of his Law is satisfied and fulfilled truly *in us*.[47]

Fourth, God's love for all Christians remains the same regardless of their obedience or lack thereof. Fifth, assurance of justification should not be discerned by one's sanctification. And sixth, God sees no sin in believers.[48]

These antinomian errors did not go unchallenged in England. Many scholars and pastors with "international reputations" wrote abun-

42. Jones, *Antinomianism*, 7; Como, "Antinomianism," 305. Young, "Antinomianism," 276, lists the following books written by these men: *Christ Alone Exalted* (Crisp, 1643); *Honey-combe of Free Justification* (Eaton, 1642); *Free Grace* (Saltmarsh, 1645); *Assertion of Grace* (Towne, 1644). Baker, "Sola Fide," 119, shows how Traske, *Treatise of Liberty from Judaism* (1620), espoused antinomian ideas.
43. Jones, *Antinomianism*, 7. Jones also notes that these antinomians were united in viewing themselves as defenders of the Reformed theological tradition.
44. Como, "Antinomianism," 306.
45. Murray, "Antinomianism," 15; Como, "Antinomianism," 306.
46. Murray, "Antinomianism," 13.
47. John Eaton, *The Honey-combe of Free Justification by Christ Alone* (London: R. B., 1642), 288 (emphasis original).
48. Jones, *Antinomianism*, 8–9. These final three ideas are all listed by Jones, and they arise from a summary of the polemical works written against antinomian teaching in the first half of the seventeenth century.

dant refutations, including Thomas Goodwin (1600–1680), Thomas Gataker (1574–1654), Samuel Rutherford (1600–1661), Thomas Shepard (1605–1649), and Anthony Burgess (1600–1663).[49] The most well-known works among these writers included Gataker's *God's Eye on His Israel* (1644), Rutherford's *Trial and Triumph of Faith* (1645), and Burgess's *Vindiciae Legis* (1646).[50]

Antinomianism in New England

The seeds of antinomian teaching in Puritan England, along with the insidious influence of Familism, bore heretical fruit in the American colonies as supporters of these ideas shipped across the Atlantic to the New World. The most famous of these supporters included Anne Hutchinson (1591–1643), wife of prominent Boston citizen William Hutchinson and mother of fifteen; Henry Vane, governor of Massachusetts from May 1636–August 1637; and two pastors, John Wheelwright (ca. 1592–1679) and John Cotton (1585–1652).[51] They would all play a part in the antinomian debates of 1636–1638, which have been called "the first and probably also the most threatening crisis of American [church] history."[52]

The central figure of the antinomian controversy was Anne Hutchinson, whose influence through Bible studies in her home and counsel given to the women of Boston and its surrounding towns had a significant impact on the churches of New England. As concern grew among the pastors of the colony, a meeting of the General Court was convened

49. Jones, *Antinomianism*, 8.
50. Young, "Antinomianism," 276.
51. Jones, *Antinomianism*, 9; Murray, "Antinomianism," 10–25. We should note that Cotton's main involvement in the controversy arose from positive comments Anne Hutchinson made about him as he served as her pastor in Boston from 1634–1638. Cotton never supported her teaching once he realized the extent of her heretical thinking, and he presided over her excommunication from the church in March 1638. See Murray, "Antinomianism," 30–68, for a thorough defense of Cotton's orthodoxy in the controversy. Though Wheelwright did support Anne early in the controversy (he was the only pastor to disagree with the 1637 synod's conclusions that Anne was teaching heresy) and though he was also banished from the colony, he did come to his senses (in Cotton Mather's words) seven years later. At that point he was restored to ministry and remained a faithful pastor until he died in 1679 (Murray, 19–29).
52. Van den Brink, "Calvin, Witsius, and the English Antinomians," 232. Murray, "Antinomianism," 29, states, "And lest there be any doubt whether the subject is worth this degree of attention let it be remembered that the great dispute of the years 1636–38 wa]s not over some incidental, secondary issue. It concerned the final destinies of men. . . . That being so, the churches of America never had a more important controversy."

in December 1636. The general viewpoint of all but Wheelwright and Cotton was that the "new opinions" being taught by Hutchinson and others were greatly troubling.[53]

Antinomian teaching continued to increase and created the need for a church synod meeting, the first in New England's history, in August 1637. At least twenty-five ministers and members of their churches met to debate and condemn a list of eighty-two errors that had become common themes of antinomian teaching.[54] During the three-week meeting, John Cotton came to realize that a number of the members of his church, who were messengers at the synod, "leaned to Mrs. Hutchinson" in their beliefs and withdrew from the meeting. Greatly disappointed, Cotton sided with the majority in condemning the antinomian errors, stating, "To clear myself, and the sounder members of our church from partaking in those manifold errors presented, I declared my judgment openly before all the assembly, 'That I esteemed some of the opinions to be blasphemous; some of them heretical; many of them erroneous; and almost all of them incommodiously expressed.'"[55] The only minister to disagree with the findings of the synod was John Wheelwright.[56]

While the Synod's conclusions were clearly stated, the main proponent of the antinomian heresy, Anne Hutchinson, had yet to be confronted. So the General Court convened in November 1637 to investigate her beliefs. The trial lasted two days and concluded with a vote, supported by all but three members, to banish Mrs. Hutchinson from the colony due to her antinomian teaching.[57] She was confined to her home in Boston until the spring, when she would be required to move, but this did not thwart her ongoing insistence to spread her doctrine. Finally, in March 1638, her church in Boston excommunicated her, as described by Cotton: "With common consent both of the Elders and Brethren of our church, she was cast out of our communion."[58]

---

53. Murray, "Antinomianism," 18.
54. John Winthrop, *Short Story*, 1–19.
55. John Cotton, *The Way of Congregational Churches Cleared* (London: Matthew Simmons, 1648), 48.
56. Murray, "Antinomianism," 24. Wheelwright's stance at the synod resulted in his removal from the colony by order of the General Court in November 1637.
57. Murray, "Antinomianism," 25–26.
58. Cotton, *The Way Cleared*, 61.

The tenets of antinomian teaching espoused by Mrs. Hutchinson and her followers included the ideas that sanctification should not be seen as giving evidence of true belief and that Christians are not bound to the law as a rule of life.[59] Joseph Felt provides a list of several more antinomian statements condemned by the synod:

> [1] If I be holy, I am never the better accepted by God; if I be unholy, I am never the worse: this I am sure of, he that hath elected me must save me. [2] If Christ will let me sin, let him look to it; upon his honour be it. [3] There is a great stir about graces and looking to hearts; but give me Christ; I seek not for graces, but for Christ. . . . I seek not for sanctification, but for Christ; tell me not of meditation and duties, but tell me of Christ. [4] I may know I am Christ's not because I do crucify the lusts of the flesh, but because I do not crucify them, but believe in Christ that crucified my lusts for me. [5] If Christ be my sanctification, what need I look to anything in myself, to evidence my justification?[60]

Polemical writings that sought to address New England's antinomian teaching included John Cotton's *The Way of Congregational Churches Cleared* (1648), Thomas Hooker's *The Application of Redemption* (1656), and Edward Johnson's *Wonder-Working Providence of Sion's Saviour in New England* (1654). Other contributors included Thomas Shepard (1605–1649), John Winthrop (1588–1649), and John Wilson (1588–1667).

Antinomianism in Nonconforming England

Antinomianism raised its head again, emerging as one of several debates among nonconformists in the years following the Civil War and the Great Ejection of 1662. Samuel Crisp's reprint of the sermons of his father, Tobias Crisp (*Christ Alone Exalted* in 1690), served as the catalyst that sparked the controversy.[61] The book was endorsed

59. Murray, "Antinomianism," 27.
60. Joseph B. Felt, *The Ecclesiastical History of New England*, 2 vols. (Boston: Congregational Library Association, 1855), 1:318.
61. Michael A. G. Haykin, "'War with the Hydra of Antinomianism': The English Baptist Tradition and the Pursuit of Holiness, 1630s–1830s," *JETS* 66.3 (2023): 543; Jones, *Antinomianism*, 11.

by a prominent Particular Baptist Hanserd Knollys (1599–1691) and prompted several Congregationalist writers to voice their support.[62] These included Isaac Chauncy (1632–1712),[63] Richard Davis,[64] and Robert Traill.[65] Chauncy coined the term "neonomian" to describe opponents like Daniel Williams who spoke of duties of the gospel as well as conditions for salvation.[66]

The main issues of contention during this nonconformist controversy included the following antinomian beliefs: (1) any place given to human activity in the order of salvation leads back to Rome, (2) there is an absolute contrast between law and gospel since the law commands to do and the gospel forbids to do anything,[67] (3) the indicatives of justification lead to the virtual elimination of the imperative to walk in the Spirit,[68] and (4) a strong emphasis on the substitution of Christ and the believer results in the notion that the sinners' sinful deeds are considered as performed by Christ whereas his passion and action is their righteousness.[69]

The reprinting of Tobias Crisp's antinomian sermons had an opposite response from several nonconformists of both Presbyterian and Baptist persuasion. Richard Baxter (1615–1691) was loudest among these voices, though he died shortly after the book's publication.[70] Picking up Baxter's mantle was his friend, Daniel Williams (ca. 1643–1716) who stated, "True holiness, sincere obedience, or good works, and

62. Haykin, "Hydra of Antinomianism," 543.
63. Isaac Chauncy, *Neonomianism Unmask'd: or the Ancient Gospel Pleaded, Against the Other, Called a New Law or Gospel* (London: J. Harris at the Harrow in the Poultry, 1692). Chauncy wrote this book as a response to Daniel Williams's book *Gospel-Truth Stated and Vindicated* (1692).
64. Jones and Ramsey, "Antinomian-Neonomian Controversy," 24. Apparently, Davis was a controversial character whose antinomian teaching prompted him to lose financial support from the Common Fund in 1692.
65. Traill published an anonymous response against Williams entitled *A Vindication of the Protestant Doctrine Concerning Justification, and of its Preachers and Professors from the unjust charge of Antinomianism* in 1692. Jones and Ramsey, "Antinomian-Neonomian Controversy," 24–25, describe this work as "shorter and less sharp than Chauncy's, [though] it still packed a punch."
66. Jones, *Antinomianism*, 10. In modern parlance the label "neonomian" would be parallel to "legalist."
67. Van den Brink, "Calvin, Witsius, and the English Antinomians," 232, delineates these first two beliefs.
68. Haykin, "Hydra of Antinomianism," 544.
69. Van den Brink, "Calvin, Witsius, and the English Antinomians," 233.
70. Haykin, "Hydra of Antinomianism," 543; Jones, *Antinomianism*, 11–12, considers Baxter's participation in the debate as "unfortunate for those who claimed to be orthodox, because his doctrine of justification was not orthodox."

perseverance, are the way to heaven, and so necessary to the salvation of a believer that without them he cannot be saved, and continuing in them he shall be saved."[71] A few less controversial respondents to antinomian teaching included John Flavel (ca. 1627–1691), John Owen (1616–1683), and Benjamin Keach (1640–1704).[72] One final writer whose attempts to offer a mediating position ended up supporting an anti-antinomian position was Dutch theologian Herman Witsius. Apparently, proponents from both sides of the antinomian debate appealed to Witsius for support of their position.[73] In his response, Witsius accepted the antinomian insistence on God's free grace, but he acknowledged that there are still many imperatives for believers to obey that are not fulfilled substitutionarily by Christ.[74]

Eighteenth Century

The vestiges of antinomian teaching continued into the eighteenth century despite the valiant efforts of many good theologians in the previous century. Because of these antinomian fumes in the air, the environment was ripe for theological storms to erupt. Our study concentrates on two locations: a Scottish controversy in the first quarter of the century and an English one in the last quarter of the century.

The Marrow Controversy of Scotland (1718–1726)

What many now consider to be the first major antinomian debate of the eighteenth century has ironically (in hindsight) proven to be not so antinomian after all.[75]

71. Daniel Williams, *Gospel-Truth Stated and Vindicated. Wherein some of Dr. Crisp's Opinions Are Considered; and the Opposite Truths Are Plainly Stated and Confirmed*, 3rd ed. (London: John Lawrence, 1698), 132. Haykin, "Hydra of Antinomianism," 543.
72. Jones and Ramsey, "Antinomian-Neonomian Controversy," 23; Haykin, "Hydra of Antinomianism," 543. Keach wrote a fifty-page response against the antinomians in 1698 entitled *A Medium betwixt two Extremes*.
73. Van den Brink, "Calvin, Witsius, and the English Antinomians," 233. Witsius's *Animaadversiones irenicae* was published in 1696.
74. Van den Brink, "Calvin, Witsius and the Antinomians," 233.
75. This is the judgment of several historians who consider the theology of Thomas Boston and James Hog and other "marrow men" to be orthodox and not antinomian. See Jones, *Antinomianism*, 13–16; Ferguson, *The Whole Christ*, 33–36 (defending the "marrow men" against the accusation of antinomianism is one of the major burdens of Ferguson's book); William VanDoodewaard, "The Marrow Controversy," in *A New Divinity: Transatlantic Reformed Evangelical Debates during the Long Eighteenth Century*, ed. Mark Jones and Michael A. G. Haykin (Göttingen: Vandenhoeck & Ruprecht, 2018), 38–41.

The Marrow Controversy began with the reprinting of a little known book, *The Marrow of Modern Divinity*, that was originally published in two parts by "E. F.": part one in 1645 and part two in 1649.[76] Subsequent study has determined that E. F. was Edward Fisher, a barber surgeon from London who died in 1650.[77] The book was written in a dialogue format with four participants: (1) Neophytus, a young Christian troubled about elements of gospel truth; (2) Evangelista, the pastor who counsels him; (3) Nomista, a legalist; and (4) Antinomista, an antinomian.[78] Fisher's stated goal was "to walk as a middle man betwixt them both, in showing to each of them his erroneous path (which is Jesus Christ received truly, and walked in answerably), as a means to bring them both unto him, and make them both one in him."[79] He wanted to write because "both these paths [legalism and antinomianism] leading from Christ, have been justly judged as erroneous."[80] The *Marrow* was quite popular and went through nine editions by 1699, but it fell into obscurity until Scottish minister James Hog reprinted the first part in 1717 and John Williamson reprinted the second part in 1718.[81]

At this stage the Scottish antinomian debate began in earnest. Critics of *The Marrow of Modern Divinity* were not timid in using the antinomian label when offering their evaluations of the book.[82] Pamphlets by the "marrow brethren" defending their doctrine were, in turn, answered by opponents, and so on. The uproar advanced to the level of the General Assembly meeting of the Scottish Presbyterian Church in 1719 when the Commission for Purity of Doctrine was tasked with

76. Ferguson, *Whole Christ*, 33. The most thorough discussion of the very complicated publishing history of *Marrow* is by William VanDoodewaard, "A Journey into the Past: The Story of *The Marrow of Modern Divinity*," in Edward Fisher, *The Marrow of Modern Divinity* (Fearn: Christian Focus, 2009), 21–32. This excellent reprint of Fisher's original work also includes: (1) Thomas Boston's notes that were added to *The Marrow* in its Scottish edition published in 1726, (2) an appendix by John Brown of Haddington [1722–1787] that gives answers to twelve questions raised by the General Assembly of 1720 against the *Marrow*, and (3) an introduction by Philip Graham Ryken. All references in this essay will be taken from this Christian Focus edition.

77. VanDoodewaard, "Journey into the Past," 22–28.

78. Ferguson, *Whole Christ*, 33.

79. Fisher, *Marrow*, 42.

80. Fisher, *Marrow*, 42.

81. VanDoodewaard, "Journey into the Past," 28–29.

82. James Hadow, *The Antinomianism of the Marrow of Modern Divinity Detected* (Edinburgh: John Mosman, 1721) cited in VanDoodewaard, "The Marrow Controversy," 46.

examining the matter. The commission's decision culminated in the Act of the Assembly in 1720, which strictly prohibited and discharged all ministers to "warn and exhort their people, in whose hands the said book is, or may come, not to read or use the same."[83]

The *Marrow's* supporters responded with answers to twelve questions posed by the 1720 act, and these were given to the 1721 assembly, which referred the issue to a commission that would give a response to the 1722 General Assembly. Unsurprisingly, the 1722 decision merely confirmed the declaration of 1720, and the Marrow men felt that their concerns were never truly answered.[84]

VanDoodewaard provides a helpful summary of the three main areas of theological dispute during the Marrow Controversy: (1) preparationism versus preparatory grace, (2) the relationship of saving faith and assurance, and (3) the gospel offer.[85] None of these relate directly to antinomian teaching except, perhaps, the second area. And in regard to assurance, the Marrow supporters held to both objective and subjective aspects of assurance tied to saving faith, a viewpoint that antinomians would have denied.[86]

Even though Edward Fisher may have stated things a little too strongly (for some) in regard to the free offer of the gospel, the charge of antinomianism leveled by such detractors as James Hadow and his supporters in the General Assembly is unsupportable and should have been judged so in the 1720s.[87] This is clear in light of Fisher's own statements in part one of the *Marrow* and even clearer in part two, "which is wholly taken up in the manifestation of the obligation, meaning, and advantage of observing the law of God."[88] In his introduction to the twelve questions that the Marrow men presented to the General Assembly in 1720, John

83. VanDoodewaard, "Journey into the Past," 30.
84. Ferguson, *Whole Christ*, 34; VanDoodewaard, "Journey into the Past," 30. The answers to the twelve queries are included in an appendix in Fisher, *Marrow*, 346–76. Incidentally, there was a group of twelve ministers who formulated answers to the twelve queries. Chief among them was Thomas Boston; and others were James Hog, James Wardlaw, and brothers Ralph and Ebenezer Erskine (Ferguson, *Whole Christ*, 34).
85. VanDoodewaard, "The Marrow Controversy," 45–53.
86. VanDoodewaard, "The Marrow Controversy," 50–51.
87. VanDoodewaard, "Journey into the Past," 30–31.
88. John Brown, "Appendix," in *The Marrow of Modern Divinity*, 345. John Brown of Haddington (1722–1787) wrote the introductory words (from which this citation is taken) to this delineation of the twelve questions with answers and explanations for each one that the Marrow supporters gave to the General Assembly in 1720.

Brown of Haddington gives a list of antinomian teachings then present in England which the second part of the *Marrow* most certainly denied. The teachings included: (1) believers are not under the law, (2) believers do not commit sin because the Lord sees no sin in them, (3) God cannot be angry with believers, and (4) the moral law is not a binding rule of duty for the Christian.[89] Even though the Marrow men cannot rightly be charged with promoting antinomian doctrine, concerns about antinomianism and legalism in England and Scotland in the eighteenth century were not unfounded as we shall see in the next section.

Antinomianism in England

While the smoldering wick of antinomian doctrine in the first quarter of eighteenth century in Scotland appears to have died out by the middle 1700s, the pesky antinomian embers left over from the previous century fueled a resurgence of antinomian teaching in England during the last half of the 1700s. John Wesley accused two Methodist pastors, James Relly (1721/22–1778) and Roger Balls, of teaching antinomian doctrine.[90] Additionally, a pair of Anglican ministers were known for trumpeting antinomian principles: John Bradford (1750–1805) at Birmingham and Thomas Pentycross (1748–1808) at Wallingford.[91] Baptists did not escape unscathed either, as William Augustus Clarke, a Particular Baptist pastor in London, taught and practiced antinomianism.[92]

But by far the most notorious purveyor of antinomian doctrine was an Independent minister named William Huntington (1745–1813). His pastoral ministry spanned thirty-six years, thirty of which were in the West End of London, where he experienced "a prominence which no other minister of similar [antinomian] views had ever enjoyed."[93]

89. Brown, "Appendix," 345–46.
90. Oliver, *History*, 114–15. An example of Relly's antinomian tendencies can be found in a statement by James Relly, *Christian Liberty, or the Liberty Wherewith Christ Has Made Us Free* (London: M. Lewis, 1775), 12, "From the decalogue, or moral law, . . . hath Christ also set us free."
91. Oliver, *History*, 142–43.
92. Haykin, "Hydra of Antinomianism," 547, quotes a letter from John Rippon to William Rogers in which Rippon describes Clarke (who pastored 1773–1792), as "an Antinomian in doctrine & practice [who] for a considerable time past, till he left this country, has lived in adultery so notoriously that his own dearest friends were forced to abandon him."
93. Oliver, *History*, 120. Oliver, 176, cites a number of polemical works Huntington wrote that not only attacked his theological enemies but also revealed his antinomian beliefs. These included *Letter to the Rev. Caleb Evans* (1789), *The Broken Cistern and the Springing Well* (1791 against John Ryland Sr.), and *Excommunication* (1791 against John Ryland Jr. and

Huntington's antinomian doctrine included several tenets that seem to have been common among all antinomians of his day: (1) the moral law is not a rule of life for the believer;[94] (2) assurance of salvation is based on personal experience rather than divine promises or obedience;[95] (3) a passive doctrine of sanctification;[96] (4) a low view of sin in the believer's life;[97] and (5) a belief that the Christian cannot grieve/displease the Spirit.[98] A sixth characteristic of antinomian teaching came from an eyewitness observation provided by Andrew Fuller, who heard a preacher say, "The new nature is not touched or sullied by [my overwhelming lusts and corruptions]: it cannot sin, because it is born of God—I stand amidst this overwhelming sea unhurt."[99]

Although many orthodox pastors and parishioners responded to the antinomian threat, the best known among them was Andrew Fuller (1754–1815).[100] Abraham Booth's *The Death of Legal Hope* (1770),

Andrew Fuller). Another example is William Huntington, *The Moral Law Not Injured by the Everlasting Gospel. A Sermon, Preached in Substance at Providence Chapel; and Humbly Addressed to the Rev. Rowland Hill* (London, 1791).

94. Haykin, "Hydra of Antinomianism," 549; Oliver, *History*, 123–24.

95. Oliver, *History*, 126, 130.

96. Oliver, *History*, 127. In referring to Huntington's view as "passive," Oliver means that Huntington's writings speak of sanctification as a monergistic work with God being the cause of the believer's obedience, while the believer is not the active agent of good works. This work of God in sanctification is based on the premise that it is God's will of decree rather than his will of command from which sanctification springs and is accomplished. This is why Huntington's preaching lacked any mention of Christian duty: "He preached on doctrinal and experiential themes to the exclusion of practical ones" (140).

97. Maria de Fleury, *Antinomianism Unmasked and Refuted* (London: T. Wilkins, 1791), 13. This low view of sin was manifested by the following ideas: (1) sorrow for sin is unnecessary, (2) God never chastises for sin, and (3) heart holiness is not something believers should be concerned about. Furthermore, "Some have even gone so far as to say, they could not sin, because there was no sin to a believer."

98. De Fleury, *Antinomianism Unmasked*, 13; Haykin, "Hydra of Antinomianism," 548–51. Haykin cites John Ryland Jr.'s understanding of grieving the Holy Spirit not only to include the idea of displeasing the Spirit but also the failure to love holiness and live obediently; he gives this summary of Ryland's view: "In sum, salvation by the Spirit's grace alone and a life of good works, the fruit of his indwelling presence—'evangelical religion and holy practice'—are 'inseparably connected'" (551).

99. Andrew Fuller, "Picture of an Antinomian," in *The Complete Works of Andrew Fuller*, ed. Joseph Belcher, 3 vols. (Harrisonburg, VA: Sprinkle, 1988), 3:829–31.

100. Haykin, "Hydra of Antinomianism," 546–47, calls Fuller "The most important divine in the transatlantic Baptist world at the close of the eighteenth century and throughout the century that followed." Oliver, *History*, 118–19, states that one of the major problems frequently referenced in Fuller's correspondence was the spread of antinomianism. Apparently, Fuller was working on a book about antinomianism that was uncompleted at the time of his death (141).

Maria de Fleury's *Antinomianism Unmasked* (1791), and Caleb Evans's *Circular Letter of the Western Association* (1789) were notable contributions in the battle against antinomianism. Other apologists included John Ryland Sr. (1723–1792), Rowland Hill (1744–1833), John Rippon (1751–1836), and Robert Hall Jr. (1764–1831).[101]

Nineteenth Century

The furious conflict against antinomianism that began in the last quarter of the eighteenth century continued into the next as William Huntington and those who followed in his train continued their antinomian teaching and writing. Two of Huntington's followers were Anglicans: Robert Hawker (1753–1827) and William J. Brook (who seceded from the church and became an Independent in 1805).[102] Several Baptists followed Huntington's teachings including Washington Wilkes (*A Fearless Defence of the Leading Doctrines Preached and Received by Modern Antinomians*, 1830), John Warburton (*Mercies of a Covenant God*, 1859), Joseph Philpot (1802–1869), and most prominently, William Gadsby (1773–1844).[103]

Gadsby spent his pastoral ministry in Manchester and London and was considered by many as Huntington's successor in the antinomian controversy. This was largely due to his book *The Gospel, the Believer's Rule of Conduct*, first published in 1804 with two more editions, the last appearing in 1821.[104] While Gadsby's antinomianism could be considered more moderate than Huntington's,[105] he certainly did not avoid the fray, publishing *The Present State of Religion, or, What Are the People Miscalled Antinomians?* in 1808, *The Perfect Law of Liberty* (n.d.) and *'Doctrinal Antinomianism Refuted' Entangled in Its Own Maze* in 1809 (written as a response to John Stevens's *Doctrinal Antinomianism Refuted*).[106]

101. These last three authors could easily be included in our treatment of nineteenth century antinomians since their efforts bridged the two centuries in which they lived.
102. Oliver, *History*, 143–44; Hawker actually embraced the antinomian label.
103. Oliver, *History*, 183–87, 302–5.
104. Oliver, *History*, 183–87.
105. Oliver, *History*, 175, summarizes Gadsby's ministry: "Gadsby proved to be a powerful controversialist, opposing the teachings of Andrew Fuller and promoting some of the views of William Huntington, but without the latter's bitterness. In the face of considerable opposition, however, he was able to secure a place for modified Huntingtonian Antinomianism among the Particular Baptists."
106. Oliver, *History*, 185–86.

Nineteenth-century antinomianism adhered to five basic beliefs: (1) the law is fulfilled in and not by the Christian,[107] (2) feelings and subjective evidence are trusted more than the Bible,[108] (3) reliance on the Holy Spirit's witness to the individuals' spirits as their means of assurance,[109] (4) the denial of progressive sanctification, and (5) the denial of the believer's duty to grow in grace.[110]

The alert reader will notice a number of respondents to the antinomians in the footnotes from the previous paragraph. But several others deserve mention. Chief among the opponents of nineteenth-century antinomians is John Ryland Jr. (*Serious Remarks on the Different Representations of Evangelical Doctrine by the Professed Friends of the Gospel* [1817] and *The Practical Influence of Evangelical Religion* [1819]).[111] Others include John Stevens (*Doctrinal Antinomianism Refuted* [1809]), James Upton (*Addresses on Practical Subjects* [1812]), J. Gawthorne (*The Coincidence of Antinomianism and Arminianism* [1818]), and a little later in the century, William Palmer (*A Plain Statement; Followed by a Few Reflections upon Mr. Philpot of Stamford, as a Christian, a Preacher and a Reviewer* [1847]) and Frederick Tryon (*Old Paths and New* [1847]).[112] Other than the small blip of antinomian teaching that arose during the mid-century in the writings of Joseph Philpot,[113] the writers named here were largely successful in squelching the antinomian fervor in the first quarter of the century. This statement by Thomas Chalmers in his sermons on Romans demonstrates one informed opinion from that time period (ca. 1842): "Let

107. Oliver, *History*, 183–84, suggests that this is the basic theme of Gadsby's *The Gospel, the Believer's Rule of Conduct*.

108. Oliver, *History*, 305, describes the experience-oriented ministry of Joseph Philpot and how he was confronted by contemporaries like Frederick Tryon (*Old Paths and New*, 1847) and William Palmer (*A Plain Statement; Followed by a Few Reflections upon Mr Philpot of Stamford, as a Christian, a Preacher and a Reviewer*, 1847). Oliver, *History*, 144, also tells of William Huntington's theology that was governed more by experience than by "the objective teaching of Scripture."

109. Oliver, *History*, 143, refers in particular to the writing of Robert Hawker when making this assertion.

110. Haykin, "Hydra of Antinomianism," 549, cites John Ryland Jr. who provides these last two descriptions of antinomian doctrine in his book, *Serious Remarks on the Different Representations of Evangelical Doctrine by the Professed Friends of the Gospel* (Bristol, 1817).

111. Haykin, "Hydra of Antinomianism," 548–49.

112. Oliver, *History*, 186, 302–5.

113. Philpot's antinomian writings were written and responded to in the 1840s (Oliver, *History*, 302–7).

it never be forgotten of the Particular Baptists of England, that they form the denomination of Fuller and Carey and Ryland and Hall . . . that they have waged a very noble and successful war with the hydra of Antinomianism."[114]

Summary

By the middle of the nineteenth century the antinomian blazes of the previous two centuries had been mostly extinguished. When C. H. Spurgeon pastored in London from 1854–1892, he faced many doctrinal controversies, none of which involved antinomianism. And as the twentieth century dawned, evangelical Christians in England and the United States concentrated their efforts on the major skirmish between fundamentalists and modernists. Once that major doctrinal war was over and the fundamentalists had left the mainline denominations (ca. 1950), the seeds of less significant theological issues like antinomianism (among others) began to be planted and watered, growing into full-grown plants in the second half of the twentieth century.

THE TENETS OF ANTINOMIAN TEACHING

In order to summarize the tenets of antinomian teaching I have chosen primarily to limit the sources used in this endeavor to three books,[115] three journal articles,[116] and three encyclopedia entries.[117] Summarizing the descriptions of antinomianism given in these resources as well as gleaning from the findings of our historical survey, six general characteristics of antinomian teaching come to the forefront.

1. Regarding the law: The moral law has no role in the believer's life. Taking a chapter out of Luther's theology,[118] antinomians drew a strong

114. Thomas Chalmers, *Lectures on the Epistle of Paul to the Romans* (New York: Robert Carter & Brothers, 1859), 76. Haykin, "Hydra of Antinomianism," 551, should be credited for pointing me to this citation.
115. Ferguson, *Whole Christ*; Jones, *Antinomianism*; and Winthrop, *Short Story*.
116. Haykin, "Hydra of Antinomianism," 539–51; Murray, "Antinomianism"; and van den Brink, "Calvin, Witsius, and the English Antinomians."
117. Como, "Antinomianism," 305–7; Fackre, "Antinomianism," 27; Young, "Antinomianism," 270–78.
118. See the material on the sparks of antinomianism presented earlier in the chapter. Van den Brink, "Calvin, Witsius, and the English Antinomians," 235, states, "During the 1640s Luther was by far the antinomians' greatest champion."

contrast between law (given for the sinner) and gospel (given for the Christian).[119] The emphasis on the grace of the gospel in the believer's life means that there are no duties for obedience because such calls would imply that the believer is not resting in grace.[120]

Several ramifications attend this strong de-emphasis on the role of law (or calls for obedience) in the believer's sanctification. First, the law is abrogated or set aside for the believer.[121] Second, the exercise of faith and repentance are unnecessary for the Christian.[122] Third, the teaching of the law is not necessary for guidance in the Christian life because the Spirit now rules the believer's life—in fact, the Spirit does his greatest work in saints' lives "when they endeavor least."[123]

2. Regarding the effects of justification: God sees no sin in the justified. Some antinomians held to the doctrine of eternal justification, which resulted in the "defence of a scandalous life."[124] Eternal justification teaches that "the elect are actually justified before they believe, even from all eternity."[125] The unintended consequence of such doctrine (unintended, that is, for theologians like John Gill) was that some

119. Van den Brink, "Calvin, Witsius, and the English Antinomians," 232, "Since the Law commands to do, [the antinomians] concluded that the gospel, by definition, forbids to do anything." Jones, *Antinomianism,* 126, asserts that antinomian theology believes in a "radical opposition between the law and the gospel, whereby the law only commands and the gospel only promises."

120. Fackre, "Antinomianism," 27; Young, "Antinomianism," 271, "The law is made void by grace."

121. Ferguson, *Whole Christ,* 141.

122. Young, "Antinomianism," 271. He also states that antinomians believe that they have no need to mortify sin since Christ has already mortified it for them. Furthermore, they should not "be distressed in conscience upon backsliding, but . . . should hold fast to a full assurance of . . . salvation in the midst of the vilest of sins."

123. Winthrop, *Short Story,* 11; Ferguson, *Whole Christ,* 141; Fackre, "Antinomianism," 27.

124. Haykin, "Hydra of Antinomianism," 546. Haykin indicates that John Gill held to this doctrine but was not himself antinomian. Rather, his advocacy of this teaching did lead others to adopt antinomian practices. To confirm Gill's denial of antinomianism, see Thomas J. Nettles, *By His Grace and for His Glory: A Historical, Theological, and Practical Study of the Doctrines of Grace in Baptist Life* (Grand Rapids: Baker Academic, 1986), 91–94. Thanks to Matt Shrader for pointing me to this resource.

125. Fackre, "Antinomianism," 27; Timothy George, "John Gill," in *Theologians of the Baptist Tradition,* rev. ed., ed. Timothy George and David S. Dockery (Nashville: Broadman & Holman, 2001), 26. Gill defended this teaching by saying that faith was the effect and not the cause of justification. He asserts: "The reason why we are justified is not because we have faith, but the reason why we have faith is because we are justified" (John Gill, *The Doctrine of God's Everlasting Love to His Elect, and Their Eternal Union with Christ* [London, 1752], 40; cited in George, "John Gill," 26).

thought of themselves as actually justified regardless of their personal response to the gospel.[126]

Holding to such a perspective on the doctrine of justification resulted in several antinomian ideas. (1) God sees no sin in the justified.[127] (2) If God sees no sin, then "believers [are] in some sense rendered perfect, indeed divine, in this life."[128] (3) Furthermore, the moral law should not be seen as a pattern for the Christian life because it actually undervalues the imputation of Christ's righteousness.[129] (4) Ultimately when sin in the believer's life is devalued in this way, holiness or unholiness of life does not matter.[130]

3. Regarding sanctification: Stress the indicatives and deny or minimize the imperatives. Antinomians were reticent to call Christians to personal holiness. Ferguson describes antinomian doctrine: "Divine indicatives so overwhelmed divine imperatives that biblical balance was lost."[131] In some cases the pendulum had not only swung toward an indicative emphasis—antinomians had reached the end of the scale and virtually eliminated the imperatives altogether.[132]

For the antinomian, the indicatives of Scripture provided reasons why the imperatives should be minimized or dismissed. These included union with Christ, substitutionary atonement, and justification (in particular the imputation of Christ's holiness).[133] This overemphasis on the indicatives in sanctification had several implications, including (1) the exclusion of good works from the *ordo salutis*,[134] (2) the passivity of

126. George, "John Gill," 27.
127. Jones, *Antinomianism*, 127; Young, "Antinomianism," 271.
128. Como, "Antinomianism," 306.
129. Haykin, "Hydra of Antinomianism," 549. Eaton, *Honey-combe*, 288, the "Son's perfect doing all things is objectively and passively so truly *in us*, that we are made perfectly holy and righteous in the sight of God with that doing freely, and so the rigor of his Law is satisfied and fulfilled truly *in us*" (emphasis in original). See Murray, "Antinomianism," 13–14, for more discussion.
130. Jones, *Antinomianism*, 11; Fackre, "Antinomianism," 27; and Winthrop, *Short Story*, 16, "Christ's work of Grace can no more distinguish between an Hypocrite and a Saint, then the Rain that falls from Heaven, between the Just and the Unjust."
131. Ferguson, *Whole Christ*, 141.
132. Haykin, "Hydra of Antinomianism," 544; Fackre, "Antinomianism," 27.
133. Van den Brink, "Calvin, Witsius, and the English Antinomians," 232–33; Fackre, "Antinomianism," 27; Haykin, "Hydra of Antinomianism," 544.
134. Van den Brink, "Calvin, Witsius, and English Antinomians," 230. The *ordo salutis* is Latin for "order of salvation," which refers to the events that occur in the salvation of the individual (i.e., calling, regeneration, conversion, justification, adoption, sanctification,

the believer in sanctification,[135] (3) the conclusion that Christ is the sole actor in the believer's sanctification such that "any work we perform is not our work but Christ's,"[136] and (4) the belief that any concern shown in regard to holiness and good works is "legalism."[137]

4. Regarding the relationship between justification and sanctification: Blur the differences between justification and sanctification. The historic understanding of the difference between justification and sanctification relates to the truth that in justification a Christian is declared righteous apart from any doing of the works of the law while in sanctification a Christian grows in holiness through the gradual transforming work of the Spirit. Put another way, justification is *monergistic* in that God justifies apart from any work of the Christian (Rom 4:5; Gal 2:16), and sanctification is *synergistic* in that both God and the Christian work together in the growth process (Phil 2:12–13).[138]

Antinomians typically confused these two doctrines by stating that both justification and sanctification are monergistic, entirely of God's doing because of union with Christ.[139] Additionally, antinomians believed that since Christ is the believer's sanctification, it was an error to make sanctification an evidence of justification by looking at one's own spiritual fruit.[140] As a result of this type of assertion, John Winthrop states that antinomians actually de-emphasized the

perseverance, glorification). See John M. Frame, *Concise Systematic Theology*, ed. John J. Hughes (Phillipsburg, NJ: P&R Publishing, 2023), 460.

135. Como, "Antinomianism," 306; Winthrop, *Short Story*, 13, states, "A Man may not be exhorted to any duty, because he hath no power to do it."

136. Jones, *Antinomianism*, 125; van den Brink, "Calvin, Witsius, and English Antinomians," 232–33.

137. Murray, "Antinomianism," 15, "Any insistence upon duties in the Christian life had become 'legalism.'" Haykin, "Hydra of Antinomianism," 548.

138. Wayne Grudem, *Systematic Theology*, 2nd ed. (Grand Rapids: Zondervan Academic, 2020), 924–25. These distinctions have been the standard, orthodox teaching of the church for two millennia. The "sanctification" referred to in such discussions of these two doctrines would normally be labeled "progressive" sanctification as compared to "past" and "ultimate" sanctification.

139. Eaton, *Honey-combe*, 288, "By the power of his imputation, [God] doth so truly cloath us both within and without with this his Son's doing and fulfilling of the Law perfectly, that we also continue in all things to do them in the sight of God, not inherently and actively, by our own doing, but because his Sonnes perfect doing all things is objectively and passively so truly *in us*." Jones, *Antinomianism*, 29, states, "This view obliterates human responsibility [in sanctification]." Also see Murray, "Antinomianism," 13.

140. Jones, *Antinomianism*, 11; Murray, "Antinomianism," 23; Young, "Antinomianism," 272; Winthrop, *Short Story*, 15–16.

importance of fruit-bearing in sanctification, "Sanctification is so far from evidencing a good estate, that it darkens it rather; and a man may more clearly see Christ when he seeth no sanctification, than when he doth; the darker my sanctification is, the brighter is my justification."[141]

5. Regarding assurance: Obedience cannot be used as a basis for assurance. Antinomians were united in their assertion that the *only* ground for assurance was faith in God's promises.[142] Many examples could be given, but Winthrop's description of the situation is clear: "The Spirit giveth such full and clear evidence of my good estate, that I have no need to be tried by the fruits of Sanctification, this were to light a Candle to the Sun."[143] Several others affirm the "immediacy of the witness of the Holy Spirit apart from the evidences of a holy life" as the key element of assurance for the Christian apart from any reliance on good works.[144] Finally, antinomians clearly desired to ground assurance in the objective reality of the promises of God apart from any subjective reliance upon the fruit of obedience. Jones comments, "In [the antinomians'] yearning to give assurance of salvation to their people, they stripped away a number of biblical truths and attempted to give justification by faith an all-controlling place in the life of the Christian."[145]

6. Regarding the love of God: The benevolent and complacent love of God are one and the same. When speaking about God's love for His children, theologians typically speak of two major components of that love: (1) God's benevolent love shown in his election and predestination—an unconditional love; and (2) God's complacent love displayed in his pleasure or displeasure toward his children in accordance with their holiness—a conditional love.[146] Antinomians typically collapsed

141. Winthrop, *Short Story*, 17.

142. Jones, *Antinomianism*, 127.

143. Winthrop, *Short Story*, 16.

144. Ferguson, *Whole Christ*, 142; Murray, "Antinomianism," 46; Young, "Antinomianism," 272.

145. Jones, *Antinomianism*, 127. By confounding justification and sanctification so much, the antinomians insisted that "true sanctification is nothing but believing the gospel more and more" (27). And basing assurance so completely on the objective truth of justification had this effect: "At bottom, the solution to the problem of assurance was to believe in our justification more" (99). Young, "Antinomianism," 272.

146. Jones, *Antinomianism*, 83–87. Distinguishing between the benevolent and complacent love of God may have "a rich Reformed pedigree" (84), but the concept still calls for further

these two kinds of love by denying the concept of God's complacent or contingent love.[147] Mark Jones provides several examples of antinomian writers who were happy to affirm such statements as this: "If I be holy, I am never the better accepted of God; if I be unholy, I am never the worse: this I am sure of, he that hath elected me must save me."[148]

SUMMARY

Our survey of antinomianism has revealed six general characteristics:

1. the moral law has no role in the believer's life;
2. God sees no sin in those who are justified;
3. teaching on sanctification stresses the indicatives and denies or minimizes the imperatives;
4. there is a blurring of the differences between justification and sanctification;
5. obedience cannot be used as a basis for assurance; and
6. the benevolent and complacent love of God for the Christian are one and the same.

In delineating these six general characteristics of antinomianism, it is necessary to note that people did not need to hold to all six of

explanation. First, in regard to terminology, love as *complacent* (an archaic term) should be replaced with love as *affection, pleasure, approval*, or even better, *contingent* (I thank my wife, Elaine, for suggesting these improved terms). Second, in regard to the concept, a comparison of the two loves of God with the distinction between the two wills of God in the doctrine of providence may give clarity to this discussion. John Piper, "Are There Two Wills in God?" in Schreiner and Ware, *Still Sovereign*, 109, explains, "Theologians have spoken of sovereign will and moral will, efficient will and permissive will, secret will and revealed will, will of decree and will of command, decretive will and preceptive will, *voluntas signi* (will of sign) and *voluntas beneplaciti* (will of good pleasure)." Thus, in regard to the doctrine of providence, God has an unconditional will of decree that never changes, and he has a conditional will of permission or desire that is based upon the actions of humans. In similar fashion God loves all Christians unconditionally (benevolent love) shown in his electing and saving grace, and he loves Christians conditionally (complacent or contingent love) in that he is pleased or displeased with them based on their obedience or disobedience. For example, God was displeased with the disobedient Laodicean church (Rev 3:15–16) and he calls his children to please him with their obedience (1 Thess 4:1). See Jones, *Antinomianism*, 92–95, for more examples.

147. Young, "Antinomianism," 271, explains the antinomian claim that God "is not displeased with [Christians] if they sin."

148. See Jones, *Antinomianism*, 81–96, for a listing of antinomian examples. Felt, *Ecclesiastical History*, 1:318, provides this statement along with eight others deemed "unsafe" by the synod of elders in 1637.

these characteristics to be considered members of the (hypothetical) First Order of the Antinomians. While some may have affirmed all six tenets, some may have affirmed only one—this would still qualify them as antinomian.

The goal of providing this historical survey of antinomianism from the time of the Reformation to the middle of the twentieth century has been to reveal antinomianism's general characteristics as a foundational lens through which to view the three current-day forms of antinomianism in the evangelical church. We turn now in chapter 7 to study the first of these groups: Free Grace.

CHAPTER 7

FREE GRACE AND PERSEVERANCE

INTRODUCTION

The historical study of antinomianism provided in the previous chapter serves as a basis for our next three chapters in which we consider three kinds of antinomian teaching in the modern day: Free Grace, Radical Grace, and Hyper-Grace. We will learn that all three types of antinomian teaching exalt the doctrine of grace, emphasize many of the same antinomian themes rehearsed in chapter 6, and flow out of three different models of sanctification teaching.[1]

I invite the reader to picture a large antinomian river fed by three streams. Each stream represents one of the grace groups (Free Grace, Radical Grace, and Hyper-Grace). Flowing out of the Pentecostal model of sanctification is Hyper-Grace teaching, which will be covered in chapter 9. The Reformed model of sanctification serves as the source of the Radical Grace stream and will be examined in chapter 8. And the third stream—Free Grace theology—surges out of the Chaferian model of sanctification. This third stream is the focus of attention in the present chapter. My method in this chapter and the next two follows the same basic pattern: (1) History—how did the Free Grace movement come into being? (2) Proponents—who are the voices of Free Grace theology? And (3) tenets—what beliefs do these proponents espouse? Once we have considered these important background issues related to the Free Grace movement, I discuss

1. Portions of this chapter were first published as Jon Pratt, "The Free Grace Movement and Perseverance," in *To Seek, To Do, and To Teach: Essays in Honor of Larry D. Pettegrew*, ed. Doug Bookman, Tim Sigler, and Michael Vlach (Cary, NC: Shepherds Press, 2022), 155–75. Used with permission.

how the teaching of this group relates to the doctrine of perseverance.[2] Finally, I show how Free Grace theology intersects with antinomianism and thereby falls under the condemning label of this erroneous distortion of perseverance.

THE HISTORY AND PROPONENTS OF THE FREE GRACE MOVEMENT

Precursors of the Free Grace Movement

Any movement has precursors, and there appear to be three in particular that contributed to the theology promoted by the Free Grace movement today. First, a 1959 article in *Eternity* magazine pitted Everett F. Harrison (a Dallas Seminary graduate and former professor) against John R. W. Stott (a noted British pastor and author) as they debated the question, "Must Christ be Lord to Be Savior?" Harrison took the "No" position and Stott the "Yes" position.[3] In actuality, the article was not that helpful because of the way the question was phrased. Wayne Grudem suggests it would have been much better if the questions had been, "Is repentance from sin a necessary part of saving faith?" and "Will good works and continuing to believe necessarily follow from saving faith?"[4]

Second, ten years later Charles Ryrie entered the fray by entitling one of the chapters in *Balancing the Christian Life*, "Must Christ be Lord to Be Savior?"[5] His answer? No! One writer considers Ryrie's conclusion in the chapter as drawing "a line in the sand between the lordship and non-lordship views."[6] Unfortunately, one can already see hints of the kind of inflammatory rhetoric that would permeate the lordship salvation controversy two decades later in Ryrie's evaluation of the chapter's question: "The importance of this question cannot be overestimated

2. When speaking of *how* Free Grace teaching relates to the doctrine of perseverance, I will ask whether it denies, dismisses, minimizes, or twists the Bible's teaching about perseverance.
3. "Must Christ Be Lord to Be Savior? No . . . Yes," *Eternity* 10, no. 9 (1959): 13–18, 36–37, 48.
4. Wayne Grudem, *"Free Grace" Theology: 5 Ways It Diminishes the Gospel* (Wheaton, IL: Crossway, 2016), 22–23n23. Of course, hindsight is always 20/20; no one could have predicted back in 1959 that these issues would lead to an entire theological school of thought. See also Combs, "Disjunction," *DBSJ* 6 (2001): 30.
5. Charles Ryrie, *Balancing the Christian Life* (Chicago: Moody Press, 1969), 169–81.
6. Combs, "Disjunction," 30–31.

in relation to both salvation and sanctification. The message of faith only and the message of faith plus commitment of life cannot both be the gospel; therefore, one of them is a false gospel and comes under the curse of perverting the gospel or preaching another gospel (Gal. 1:6–9), and this is a very serious matter."[7]

Third, the most significant influence on the Free Grace movement was the teaching and writing of Professor Zane Hodges (1932–2008), who taught for twenty-seven years at Dallas Theological Seminary, from 1959–1986. Wayne Grudem accurately describes the situation: "Although only a minority of Dallas Seminary professors held a Free Grace view, Zane Hodges was an exceptionally persuasive teacher, and every year some students adopted his view. Then, through these students, the Free Grace movement gained a remarkable worldwide influence, especially in discouraging Christians from including any explicit call to repentance in their presentations of the gospel."[8] Hodges, who also is well-known for his strong support of the Majority Text position in text-critical studies of the Greek NT, penned more books advocating Free Grace theology than anyone in the movement.[9] His first three books (*The Hungry Inherit* [1972], *The Gospel Under Siege* [1981], and *Grace in Eclipse* [1985]) have now been published in a single volume.[10] His contribution to the lordship debate was *Absolutely Free! A Biblical Reply to Lordship Salvation* (1989).[11] He also penned commentaries on James (1994) and the epistles of John and Hebrews in the *Bible Knowledge Commentary* (1983).[12] Shortly before his death, he published *Six Secrets to the Christian Life* (2004).[13] Following his passing, commentaries based on his class notes were published on 1 Peter (2017), 2 Peter

7. Ryrie, *Balancing*, 170.
8. Grudem, *"Free Grace" Theology*, 22.
9. See, for example, Zane C. Hodges and Arthur L. Farstad, eds., *The Greek New Testament according to the Majority Text* (Nashville: Thomas Nelson, 1982).
10. Zane C. Hodges, *The Free Grace Primer* (Denton, TX: Grace Evangelical Society, 2018).
11. Zane C. Hodges, *Absolutely Free: A Biblical Reply to Lordship Salvation* (Grand Rapids: Zondervan Academic, 1989).
12. Zane C. Hodges, *The Epistle of James: Proven Character Through Testing*, ed. Arthur L. Farstad and Robert N. Wilkin (Corinth, TX: Grace Evangelical Society, 1994, 2015); Zane C. Hodges, "Hebrews," in Walvoord and Zuck, *The Bible Knowledge Commentary*, ed. John F. Walvoord and Roy B. Zuck (Wheaton, IL: Victor Books, 1983), 777–813; and Zane C. Hodges, "1 John," "2 John," "3 John," in *The Bible Knowledge Commentary*, 881–915.
13. Zane C. Hodges, *Six Secrets of the Christian Life* (Denton, TX: Grace Evangelical Society, 2004, 2018).

(2015), Jude (2016), and Romans (2013).[14] Indeed, Hodges's influence on Free Grace theology can hardly be overstated.[15]

Two Free Grace Organizations

The Free Grace movement officially began with the establishment of the Grace Evangelical Society (GES) in 1986.[16] Its stated purpose: "To promote the clear proclamation of God's free salvation through faith alone in Christ alone, which is properly correlated with and distinguished from issues related to discipleship."[17] In order to carry out this purpose, the society produces monthly newsletters (*Grace in Focus* [bi-monthly, forty-eight-page magazine] and *Partners in Grace* [monthly, two-page newsletter]), a biannual journal (*Journal of the Grace Evangelical Society*), a podcast (Grace in Focus Radio, five days per week), and ministry tools such as tracts and follow-up materials; they also host a nonaccredited seminary and promote regional and national conferences.

In 2004 a daughter organization, the Free Grace Alliance (FGA), was established.[18] Like the GES, the FGA is "concerned about the clear understanding, presentation, and advancement of the gospel of God's Free Grace."[19] Unlike the GES, which is primarily a resource center for Free Grace materials,[20] the FGA offers membership to the alliance both for churches and individuals—whoever is willing to affirm the FGA covenant.[21] This is not to say that the FGA does not provide grace resources, for it also sells many grace-themed books, promotes national and regional conferences, and publishes a free quarterly magazine. But the FGA is truly an alliance of grace-oriented mission agen-

14. Zane C. Hodges, *1 & 2 Peter and Jude* (Denton, TX: Grace Evangelical Society, 2024); Zane C. Hodges, *Romans: Deliverance from Wrath*, introduction and selected notes by John Niemelä, ed. Robert N. Wilkin (Corinth, TX: Grace Evangelical Society, 2013, 2022).
15. Bob Wilkin, "Introduction," in Hodges, *Free Grace Primer*, 14, evaluates Hodges's influence: "It is not a stretch to suggest that the Lord raised up Zane to be the father of the modern grace movement and that these three books [*The Hungry Inherit, The Gospel Under Siege,* and *Grace in Eclipse*] were pivotal in the birth and growth of that movement."
16. See https://faithalone.org/, accessed January 5, 2025.
17. Arthur L. Farstad, "An Introduction to Grace Evangelical Society and Its Journal," *JGES* 1 (Autumn 1988): 4. Farstad was the editor of *JGES* until his death in 1998. Robert Wilkin then served as editor from 1998–2013. Ken Yates has served as editor since 2014.
18. See https://www.freegracealliance.com/, accessed January 5, 2025.
19. See https://www.freegracealliance.com/about-us/, accessed December 26, 2024.
20. This is my observation by comparing the websites of the two organizations.
21. See https://www.freegracealliance.com/contribute/, accessed December 26, 2024.

cies (e.g., Ethnos 360), evangelistic organizations (e.g., Evantell), Bible institutes (e.g., GIBS Connect Ed), accredited colleges and seminaries (e.g., Grace School of Theology), publishers (e.g., Grace Theology Press), and podcasts (e.g., *Leading Grace*).[22]

Proponents of Free Grace Theology

Significant leaders of Free Grace theology besides Hodges include Earl Radmacher (1931–2014), Arthur Farstad (1935–1998), Robert Wilkin, Charles Bing, Joseph (Jody) Dillow, David Anderson, Shawn Lazar, Ken Yates, Fred Chay, and Dennis Rokser. A perusal of the two websites of the GES and FGA will reveal most of the books and articles written by these major proponents along with several others.

THE TENETS OF FREE GRACE THEOLOGY

Though I have already hinted at a few of the main concerns of Free Grace advocates, it will be helpful to consider their specific theological viewpoints.

The Free Grace position is often described with one of these labels: *easy believism*, *anti-lordship* or *non-lordship*, or *faith alone*. While some of these appellations are fair, I am choosing to use "Free Grace," the term this group prefers when describing itself. The *great* concern that Free Grace advocates have is that God asks nothing more of us than faith when he justifies us. Specifically, by "faith alone" they mean that no other human actions accompany faith. Thus, they would argue that it is wrong to suggest that repentance from sin must accompany faith or to say that any other good works must necessarily result from faith, including the need to continue in believing.[23] Grudem summarizes four pastoral practices that flow from the Free Grace concept of "justification by faith *alone*." (1) Evangelistic messages should generally *not* include a call to repentance,

22. See https://www.freegracealliance.com, accessed December 26, 2024. Many others could be mentioned that are found under the "Resources" tab.
23. Grudem, *"Free Grace" Theology*, 20. Bob Wilkin, Executive Director of GES, directly states in a video on the home page of the GES website (https://faithalone.org/, accessed December 26, 2024) that the Free Grace movement denies perseverance, which he defines as continuing in faith and good works to the end of one's life. Rather, he argues, the only thing necessary for someone to be saved is to believe. Notice that for Free Grace thinkers justification and perseverance have no connection at all. The moment we suggest that sanctification is inevitably or necessarily tied to justification such that all true believers will persevere, we have added to faith and have therefore taken the "free" away from "grace."

i.e., a call for an inward resolve to turn away from sin. (2) We need to give assurance to people who deny their faith after sincerely believing in Christ at one time because they are likely to still be saved, and we can assure them that they are saved. (3) A professing Christian who persists in sinful conduct should not ordinarily be warned that they may not be saved; rather, we should say that the person is foolishly missing the point that they must be who they are in Christ. (4) We need not ordinarily give assurance of salvation to people based on their continued good works, because their testimony of belief is sufficient to give assurance.[24]

Some might try to explain Free Grace theology by pointing to the lordship salvation controversy and equating the beliefs of non-lordship advocates with the Free Grace position, but this would be a mistake. Earlier I mentioned the *Eternity* magazine article and the chapter in Ryrie's *Balancing the Christian Life*, both of which introduced the lordship language that came to be used.[25] But it was John MacArthur's *The Gospel according to Jesus* that led to a number of responses, both for and against the idea.[26] Perhaps the most notable among the negative responders were Zane Hodges, *Absolutely Free! A Biblical Reply to Lordship Salvation*, and Charles Ryrie, *So Great Salvation: What It Means to Believe in Jesus Christ*.[27] Positive responses included *Christ the Lord*, edited by Michael Horton and Kenneth Gentry, *Lord of the Saved: Getting to the Heart of the Lordship Debate*.[28] Further insight into the controversy could also be gained by reading three essays that appeared in the *Journal of the Evangelical Theological Society*.[29] There never was a

24. Grudem, *"Free Grace" Theology*, 21. And Free Grace advocates would not disagree with this summary.
25. Also see G. Michael Cocoris, *Lordship Salvation—Is It Biblical?* (1983; repr. by author, 2012), though most were not aware of this book before MacArthur cited it in his book (John MacArthur, *The Gospel according to Jesus* [Grand Rapids: Zondervan Academic, 1988], 29n21).
26. MacArthur, *Gospel*. See Combs, "Disjunction," 31–32; and Grudem, *"Free Grace" Theology*, 22–23, for a listing of many of the significant responses.
27. Hodges, *Absolutely Free*; Charles C. Ryrie, *So Great Salvation: What It Means to Believe in Jesus Christ* (Wheaton, IL: Victor Books, 1991).
28. Michael S. Horton, ed., *Christ the Lord: The Reformation and Lordship Salvation* (Grand Rapids: Baker Academic, 1992); Kenneth L. Gentry Jr., *The Lord of the Saved: Getting to the Heart of the Lordship Debate* (Phillipsburg, NJ: P&R, 1992).
29. John F. MacArthur Jr., "Faith according to the Apostle James," *JETS* 33 (1990): 13–34; Earl D. Radmacher, "First Response to 'Faith according to the Apostle James' by John F. MacArthur, Jr.," *JETS* 33 (1990): 35–41; Robert L. Saucy, "Second Response to 'Faith according to the Apostle James' by John F. MacArthur, Jr.," *JETS* 33 (1990): 43–47.

resolution to the lordship salvation controversy, and both groups staked their claims on either side of this basic issue: "the gospel summons sinners to yield to Christ's authority."[30] It would take a bibliography of several pages to list all of the book reviews of *The Gospel according to Jesus*, so I will not attempt to do so here. But even after thirty-seven years, the book remains in print (it is now in its third edition), an amazing statistic for a nonacademic Christian book.[31]

Returning to our discussion of Free Grace theology and its relation to the lordship salvation controversy, the question remains, "Is a 'non-lordship' position a key element of Free Grace theology?" Yes and no. On the one hand, all Free Grace teachers disagree with the main thrust of *The Gospel according to Jesus*. But on the other hand, there are many other theologians, perhaps Charles Ryrie as the most significant among them, who disagree with the main thrust of the book and who also disagree with Free Grace theology.[32] Thus, we cannot refer to non-lordship salvation as a key element of Free Grace theology.

In addition, lordship salvation language is too imprecise and unhelpful. First, John MacArthur himself disliked the term, choosing to use it only because it had become a familiar phrase in evangelicalism at the time he wrote.[33] Second, when the question is formed around the proposition that people need only to accept Jesus as Savior but not as Lord, neither side would win or lose. The Free Grace supporters would say that Jesus is Lord over the entire universe and over our lives, even though we may not perfectly submit to his lordship.[34] On the

30. MacArthur, "Faith according to James," 13. This is MacArthur's summary of *The Gospel according to Jesus*, to which he refers in the first paragraph of the essay. To be clear, the lordship advocates would agree with this simple assertion and the non-lordship advocates would strongly oppose it.

31. I commend two reviews of *The Gospel according to Jesus*: Darrell L. Bock, "A Review of *The Gospel according to Jesus*," *BSac* 146 (1989): 21–40; and Homer A. Kent, "Review Article: *The Gospel according to Jesus*," *GTJ* 10 (1989): 67–77.

32. Those who disagree with lordship salvation and who also disagree with Free Grace theology would identify with the Chaferian or Keswick models of sanctification.

33. MacArthur, *Gospel according to Jesus*, 28–29n20: "I don't like the term 'lordship salvation.' It was coined by those who want to eliminate the idea of submission to Christ from the call to saving faith, and it implies that Jesus' lordship is a false addition to the gospel. As we shall see, however, 'lordship salvation' is simply the biblical and historic doctrine of soteriology. I use the term in this volume only for the sake of argument."

34. Charles C. Bing, *Lordship Salvation: A Biblical Evaluation and Response*, Grace Life Edition (Burleson, TX: GraceLife Ministries, 1992), 167. Cf. Grudem, *"Free Grace" Theology*, 23.

other hand, non-Free Grace people would agree that our submission to Christ's lordship is never perfectly realized in this life.[35]

Earlier I suggested that the central concern of the Free Grace movement related to the concept of justification by faith alone. Wayne Grudem's assessment of how this statement is understood by all Free Grace advocates gets us to the heart of their theology: "(1) whether repentance from sin (in the sense of remorse for sin and an internal resolve to forsake it) is necessary for saving faith; and (2) whether good works and continuing to believe necessarily follow from saving faith."[36] Historic Protestantism would argue positively for both of these propositions, and Free Grace advocates would take a negative position.

In addition to these two main concerns, four additional ideas come up repeatedly in the Free Grace literature: (1) warnings about apostasy (such as those found in Hebrews) pertain to believers and the potential loss of reward, i.e., true believers can apostatize;[37] (2) salvation in James speaks of preservation from physical death rather than spiritual death;[38] (3) assurance of salvation is objective rather than subjective, which means that emphasis is placed upon the objective promises of eternal security rather than upon subjective evidences such as good works or the internal witness of the Spirit;[39] and (4) there must be a clear separation between justification and progressive sanctification.[40]

Before discussing the Free Grace approach to perseverance and assurance as it relates to growth in holiness, I believe it would be helpful to explain the relationship between dispensationalism, Chaferian sanctification, and Free Grace theology.[41] There have been too many authors both within and outside these three camps who have confused them with each other. For example, some believe that all dispensation-

---

35. MacArthur, *Gospel according to Jesus*, xiv, "No one who is saved fully understands all the implications of Jesus' lordship at the moment of conversion." Cf. Grudem, *"Free Grace" Theology*, 23.
36. Grudem, *"Free Grace" Theology*, 24.
37. Hodges, "Hebrews," 777–813.
38. Zane C. Hodges, *The Gospel Under Siege: A Study on Faith and Works* (Dallas: Redención Viva, 1981), 19–33.
39. Grace Evangelical Society website (https://faithalone.org/), accessed December 27, 2024.
40. Free Grace Alliance website (https://www.freegracealliance.com/about-us/), accessed December 27, 2024.
41. At the beginning of this chapter, I suggested that the Free Grace stream of antinomian teaching flows out of the Chaferian model of sanctification, so I am seeking to explain that connection here.

alists hold to the model of sanctification championed by Lewis Sperry Chafer, the view Ryrie called the Chaferian view.[42] But this is not at all true. If we can conceive of three concentric circles, I believe we can understand how the views of these three groups relate (see Figure 1).

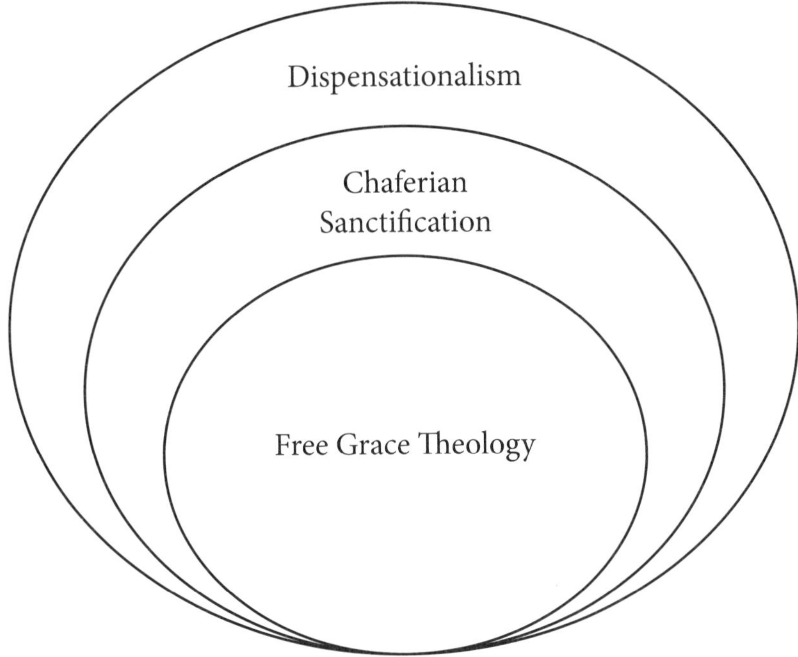

Figure 1: The Relationship Between Dispensationalism, Chaferian Sanctification, and Free Grace Theology

The first circle is the largest and includes all dispensationalists. The second, smaller circle fits entirely inside the dispensational circle—it is the Chaferian model of sanctification. Everyone who embraces the sanctification teaching of Lewis Sperry Chafer also espouses the dispensationalism Chafer taught, so all Chaferians are dispensationalists. But it is a critical error to equate the Chaferian model of sanctification with the entire system of dispensationalism, for many dispensationalists hold to

42. Charles Ryrie, "Contrasting Views on Sanctification," in *Walvoord: A Tribute*, ed. Donald K. Campbell (Chicago: Moody, 1982), 191. See Jonathan R. Pratt, "Dispensational Sanctification: A Misnomer," *DBSJ* 7 (2002): 95–108, for examples of people who have made this wrong assumption; these include John Walvoord among dispensationalists and John Gerstner among Reformed teachers. Also see Mark Snoeberger, "Second-Blessing Models of Sanctification and Early Dallas Dispensationalism," *TMSJ* 15 (2004): 93–105.

a different model of sanctification.[43] This is because dispensationalism is primarily related to eschatological and ecclesiological aspects of theology, not soteriological aspects. The third and smallest circle fits entirely within the Chaferian circle—it is the Free Grace movement. Again, this is due to the progenitor of the Free Grace group, Zane Hodges, who was a dispensationalist and who held to the Chaferian model of sanctification, especially the teaching regarding the distinction between two types of Christians—the carnal and the spiritual (i.e., those who have accepted Christ as Savior and those who have accepted Christ as Lord). Thus, everyone in the Free Grace movement would typically hold to the Chaferian model of sanctification and would also be dispensationalists. But not every Chaferian holds to Free Grace theology just as not every dispensationalist holds to the Chaferian model of sanctification.

FREE GRACE AND PERSEVERANCE

Since our focus in this chapter relates to the distortion of the doctrine of perseverance by Free Grace theology, we will not be addressing the Free Grace concern with the nature of saving faith and its relationship to repentance. Rather, we must consider how Free Grace teachers view the connection between saving faith and good works because this is the nub of the issue. Should we expect believers to persevere in faith and good works to the end of their earthly lives? The decisive answer to this question from part 1 of this book is a resounding "Yes!" But Free Grace proponents would answer negatively, so now we consider how the Free Grace teaching about assurance effectively denies the doctrine of perseverance.

The Significance of Assurance in Free Grace Theology

Why has assurance become such an important emphasis in Free Grace theology? Though there are undoubtedly a number of reasons that a diligent study of Free Grace literature might unearth, there are two in particular. First, assurance is tied to saving faith (Heb 11:1: "Faith is the

43. See Pratt, "Dispensational Sanctification," 106, for a sample list. The long list of dispensationalists who do not hold to the Chaferian model could be expanded; most of these would support the Reformed model of sanctification, with some holding to the Pentecostal or Keswick models. A significant dispensational theologian who published his systematic theology after this article and who supports the Reformed model of sanctification is McCune, *Systematic Theology*, 3:119–57.

assurance of things hoped for"), and if faith includes assurance and is a gift, then assurance is provided when faith is exercised.[44] Thus, if saving faith has transpired, assurance must be included. Second, an assured believer rests in his position and has confidence to obey God rather than living in self-condemnation because "he is never quite sure of his present standing with God."[45] Indeed, giving the believer assurance of his salvation is of utmost importance to Free Grace teachers.[46] D. A. Carson gives an excellent summary of Free Grace thinking with respect to assurance:

> [Free Grace proponents] tie assurance exclusively to saving faith, and divorce it from any support in a transformed life. The countless passages that tie genuine discipleship to obedience are handled by making a disjunction between "discipleship" passages and those that promise eternal life. Eternal life turns on faith in the saving Son of God; discipleship turns on obedience; and Christian assurance is tied only to the former. To link assurance in any way to the latter, it is argued, is to corrupt a salvation of free grace and turn it into a salvation partly dependent on works.[47]

This view of assurance that neglects the Bible's support of perseverance in favor of the desire to give certainty to people of their standing in the family of God is imbalanced and out of step with the teaching of the NT. I now offer six scriptural arguments that speak against the Free Grace view of assurance and perseverance.

Scriptural Arguments That Oppose Free Grace Assurance

The six arguments provided here are a direct response to particular claims made by Free Grace writers. Under each heading I furnish the

44. Joseph C. Dillow, *The Reign of the Servant Kings: A Study of Eternal Security and the Final Significance of Man* (Hayesville, NC: Schoettle, 1992), 288.
45. Anderson, *Free Grace Soteriology*, 205.
46. Dennis Rokser, *How NOT to Live the Christian Life by Grace: The Free Grace Faux Pas of Justification by Grace but Sanctification by Faith Plus Works* (Duluth, MN: Grace Gospel Press, 2021), 15; D. A. Carson, "Reflections on Christian Assurance," *Westminster Theological Journal.* 54 (1992): 6.
47. Carson, "Reflections, on Christian Assurance" 6. This article is the best biblical-theological treatment of assurance written in the past thirty years. Carson's insights are clear and irenic. To avoid the possibility of drowning in the details of Free Grace thinking with regard to assurance, I suggest three resources for further study: Hodges, *The Gospel Under Siege*, 9–18; Anderson, *Free Grace Soteriology*, 191–228; and Dillow, "Finding Assurance," 193–238.

Free Grace supposition followed by the scriptural rejoinder which contradicts that supposition. I am not arguing against straw men in any of these arguments, for one will find ample expression of these Free Grace ideas in the sources mentioned in notes 39 and 40 as well as many other Free Grace writings.

The Effects and Meaning of Repentance

Free Grace theology asserts that some Christians may have only an intellectual agreement with the facts of the gospel and still be truly saved. This is due to the fact that repentance refers only to a "resolve to turn from sin" with regard to the facts of the gospel.[48]

The NT epistles, however, frequently warn church attenders that some among them may not be saved because they are not producing good works—that is, their "resolve to turn from sin" was not a real change of direction. We notice that the Thessalonian believers did demonstrate real change (1 Thess 1:9: "For they themselves report concerning us the kind of reception we had among you, and how you turned to God from idols to serve the living and true God"), while other so-called believers did not validate their faith in good works and were "dead" (Jas 2:14–17). The Corinthian believers had been transformed (1 Cor 6:9–11: "and such were some of you"), and they were called to "test themselves" in order to see whether they were "in the faith" (2 Cor 13:5).[49]

Positional Truth and Fruit Bearing

Free Grace authors state, "All believers are overcomers in *position* but not necessarily in *practice*."[50] Said another way, all Christians are overcomers (Rom 8:37; Rev 2:7), but not all overcomers "walk in practical

48. David R. Anderson, "The Role of Repentance in Salvation," in Chay, *A Defense of Free Grace Theology*, 95–98. Anderson nuances this statement about mere "intellectual agreement" but in the end he does not connect repentance with justification, which he calls "relationship truth"; rather, he connects repentance with sanctification, which he calls "fellowship truth." With regard to the relationship between justification and repentance, repentance "is completely unnecessary" (98).

49. Grudem, *"Free Grace" Theology*, 80, also includes Heb 3:12; 1 John 2:3–6; 3:6, 9–10, 14. "[These] passages also challenge churchgoing people to be sure that they have genuine, saving faith, not merely superficial intellectual agreement with the facts of the gospel."

50. Dennis Rokser, Tom Stegall, and Kurt Witzig, *Should Christians Fear Outer Darkness?* (Duluth, MN: Grace Gospel Press, 2015), 423 (emphasis added). While the writers are right to affirm that all Christians are overcomers, not all Free Grace teachers concur (Dillow, *Reign of the Servant Kings*, 469–87).

victory over sin."[51] The reasons Free Grace teachers make this assertion are manifold, but the desire to provide "absolute assurance of salvation" to believers is certainly one of them.[52]

As our study in part 1 showed, however, the NT writers provide abundant evidence that all Christians are not only *positionally* sanctified but are *actually* bearing fruit. Jesus (Matt 7:17; John 15:16), Paul (Eph 2:10; Phil 2:13), Peter (1 Pet 1:8), and John (1 John 2:3–6) all affirm that every Christian is not only positionally in Christ but also perseveres in good works.[53] But not only is perseverance in good works a proof that overcomers are fruit bearers, the Bible's requirement that believers pursue holiness of life successfully is also practical evidence that their position cannot be divorced from real good works (Heb 12:14: "Strive for peace with everyone, and for the holiness without which no one will see the Lord"; 1 John 3:10: "By this it is evident who are the children of God, and who are the children of the devil; whoever does not practice righteousness is not of God, nor is the one who does not love his brother").

Spurious or False Faith

Free Grace proponents argue that a believer can actually fall away from the faith and cease believing.[54] In such cases, these types of believers are said to be carnal Christians who will be saved but will miss out on rewards at the judgment seat of Christ.

The NT writers, however recognize the existence of spurious or transitory faith. This is clear from the warnings in Hebrews; it is clear from the demand for self-examination with regard to being in the faith (2 Cor 13:5; 2 Pet 1:8–11); it is clear in the departure of false teachers from the assembly (1 John 2:19); it is clear from Jesus's description of spurious faith among his supposed followers (Matt 7:21–23; John 2:23–25; 6:66; 8:31); and it is clear from the parable of the sower,

51. Rokser, Stegall, and Witzig, *Outer Darkness*, 431.
52. Rokser, *How NOT to Live the Christian Life*, 15, asserts that it is impossible to provide "absolute assurance" to anyone who is relying on the subjectivity of seeing spiritual fruit in one's life, which is why the objective truth of one's *position* is the only true basis for assurance.
53. Jonathan R. Pratt, "The Relationship between Justification and Spiritual Fruit in Romans 5–8," *Them* 34, no. 2 (2009): 162–78.
54. Zane C. Hodges, *Absolutely Free: A Biblical Reply to Lordship Salvation*, 2nd ed. (Corinth, TX: Grace Evangelical Society, 2014), 147; Dillow, *Reign of the Servant Kings*, 311–12, states, "In remote cases it is even possible that such [regenerate] people will publicly renounce Christ and persist in either sin or unbelief to the point of physical death."

especially with regard to the second and third groups of fruitless soils (Mark 4:3–20 and parallels).[55] Furthermore, the claim that Christians can be divided into two distinct groups of spiritual and carnal believers does not hold up to the teaching of the NT.[56]

The Function of Good Works as a Basis of Assurance

The GES website states its position clearly: "Assurance of our eternal destiny is based solely on believing Jesus' promise to the believer and not on looking to our works, experiences, or behavior."[57] The important word in this statement is *solely*.[58] While some Free Grace proponents say that good works have a confirming role in assurance, the overwhelming emphasis in the literature is on the primary role of God's promises as the basis of assurance.[59] Practically speaking, Free Grace teachers deny the necessity of good works as a confirming element in providing assurance since they believe people may persist in unbelief to the point of death and still receive eternal life.[60]

The NT, however, shows that God's promises are the objective basis of assurance for believers; yet, it also shows that God uses other subjective evidences to encourage the assurance of believers.[61] These include the internal testimony of the Holy Spirit (Rom 8:15–16), evidence of inward graces (2 Pet 1:5–11), the good works that accord with genuine faith (James 2:14–26), and the reassuring evidences of faith (right belief, right behavior, right love) in 1 John.[62]

---

55. Carson, "Reflections on Christian Assurance," 13–21; McCune, *Systematic Theology*, 3:173–78.
56. Carson, "Reflections on Christian Assurance," 7–13, gives an excellent refutation of the carnal Christian teaching based on an exegesis of 1 Cor 3 and a development of how the new covenant promises apply to *all* of God's new covenant people. See also Ernest C. Reisinger, *What Should We Think of "The Carnal Christian"?* (Carlisle, PA: Banner of Truth Trust, 1978).
57. GES website (https://faithalone.org), accessed December 27, 2024.
58. Anderson, *Free Grace Soteriology*, 228, states, "We believe a person can have absolute assurance that he is born again the moment he believes. We can give him this assurance, not because of a change in his life which we can feel or see, but because we believe without doubt the promises of God which offer eternal life as a free gift to anyone who believes in Jesus Christ as the Son of God and Savior from our sins."
59. Dillow, "Finding Assurance," 203.
60. Anderson, *Free Grace Soteriology*, 203. Commenting on 2 Tim 2:12b, Anderson states, "If we deny the faith and reject Him, Christ still lives within us and cannot deny Himself, but He *will* deny our reign with Him" (emphasis original). Also see Hodges and Dillow in n54 above.
61. Schreiner and Caneday, *The Race Set Before Us*, 276; Carson, "Reflections," 3–5, 26–29; Grudem, *"Free Grace" Theology*, 87–88.
62. Second London Baptist Confession 18.2: "This certainty is not a bare conjectural and probable persuasion, grounded upon a fallible hope, but an infallible assurance of faith,

The Importance of Present Assurance

Free Grace proponents argue that "lordship salvationists"—non-Free Grace proponents—do not have any warrant for providing *present* assurance to believers because they believe in perseverance, which is naturally *future-oriented*. Thus, they essentially downplay the possibility of offering future assurance to believers based on their present obedience.[63]

Many texts, however, confirm that Christians can have *present* assurance by seeing evidences of righteous fruit in their lives (2 Pet 1:10; 1 John 2:3–6). At the same time, it is good to ask, "Why is giving personal assurance of salvation so significant to Free Grace teachers?" Carson's comment in this regard gives us a helpful perspective: "It is odd, however, that [Free Grace studies] have made personal assurance, or some peculiar understanding of it, the touchstone for the entire structure of Christian theology. The result has been truly astonishing distortions. On balance, this is a strange place to begin and end the study of theology. One might have begun with God, with Christ, with redemption, with revelation."[64]

The Mystery of Compatibilism in Sanctification

Compatibilism is the view that the following two statements are mutually compatible, despite superficial evidence to the contrary: (1) God is absolutely sovereign, but his sovereignty does not in any way mitigate human responsibility; and (2) human beings are responsible creatures, but their responsibility never serves to make God absolutely contingent.[65] This idea can be substantiated throughout Scripture, but Acts 4:27–28 is perhaps the most representative passage: "For truly in this city there were gathered together against your holy servant Jesus, whom you anointed, both Herod and Pontius Pilate, along with the Gentiles

founded on the blood and righteousness of Christ revealed in the gospel; and also upon the inward evidence of those graces of the Spirit unto which promises are made, and on the testimony of the Spirit of adoption, witnessing with our spirits that we are the children of God; and as a fruit thereof, keeping the heart both humble and holy." Also, Carson, "Reflections," 26–27; and Schreiner and Caneday, *Race Set Before Us*, 276–305.

63. Anderson, *Free Grace Soteriology*, 227, states, "Hence, *present* faithfulness is an unreliable basis for present assurance. Only *future* faithfulness can provide any grounds for assurance. But the future is always out there. Until one dies, one can always fall away. Present faithfulness is not firm footing for assurance of salvation" (emphasis in original).
64. Carson, "Reflections," 28.
65. D. A. Carson, *How Long, O Lord? Reflections on Suffering and Evil* (Grand Rapids: Baker Academic, 1990), 201.

and the peoples of Israel, to do whatever your hand and your plan had predestined to take place." This has ramifications for election, suffering, the nature of prayer, and assurance.[66]

Free Grace teachers place primary emphasis on texts that promise God's sovereign commitment to preserve his elect, while the texts that call believers to persevere in the faith are downplayed to secondary status because they seem to take away from the divine nature of the free gift of salvation.[67]

But verses like 1 Corinthians 15:10 ("But by the grace of God I am what I am, and his grace toward me was not in vain. On the contrary, I worked harder than any of them, though it was not I, but the grace of God that is with me") demonstrate the mystery of sanctification, showing the work of God to initiate the good works of evangelism and ministry in Paul's life while also affirming the personal effort, prompted by God, that Paul expended in doing the work of the ministry. With regard to the subject of assurance, Carson suggests a good way forward when considering texts that promise assurance and texts that demand perseverance: "Do warnings against apostasy function to annul the promises of God? Of course not. They are designed to promote perseverance. Do the promises of God serve to engender lethargy? Of course not. They are designed to promote zeal, gratitude, and appreciation of God's fidelity."[68]

The Relation of Free Grace Theology to Perseverance

We have learned how significant the doctrine of assurance is to Free Grace teachers in that it is: (a) tied to saving faith, and (b) is speaking of positional truth. Peeling away the layers of Free Grace teaching on assurance, we discovered six claims, each of which was refuted with scriptural evidence. These claims included: (1) repentance refers *only* to a resolve to turn away from sin, (2) absolute assurance rests on *positional* truth, (3) true believers may actually *fall away* from the faith and *cease believing*, (4) assurance is based *solely* on God's promises

66. Carson, "Reflections," 22–25.
67. Joseph Dillow, "The Role of Works in Justification," in Chay, *A Defense of Free Grace Theology*, 121–42. This entire chapter shows the inability to affirm the mystery of compatibilism in sanctification: the sovereignty of God seen in guaranteeing justification by faith alone apart from works and the responsibility of the believer to persevere in good works as a necessary result of that justification.
68. Carson, "Reflections," 26; Schreiner and Caneday, *Race Set Before Us*, 305–9.

and not on good works, (5) *present* assurance can only be provided by considering *present* promises, and (6) the mystery of God's providence in perseverance is *ignored* by emphasizing God's preserving power and minimizing the believer's duty to persevere. Taken together, these six claims point to a denial of the doctrine of perseverance by Free Grace teachers, which is why this theological perspective should be described as antinomian.[69]

Before looking at the way Free Grace theology connects with antinomianism, a few observations are needed in regard to assurance and how Free grace teachers understand it.

First, when the necessary link between justification and good works (faith and deeds of faith) is severed in the interest of giving assurance, encouragement to strive for holiness is downplayed. I am not suggesting that Free Grace teachers do not care about living holy lives, but that the drive to emphasize present, personal assurance of salvation has lent itself to an unfortunate diminishing of the importance of living obediently (1 John 2:3–6).

Second, the strong emphasis on assurance and inattention to perseverance has resulted in many unsaved people who think they are true converts. Grudem observes:

> Many of these people do not even go to church anymore, but they still think that they are saved, because, if you were to ask them, they would say that they think it is true that they are sinners in need of salvation, and they think it is true that Jesus died to pay for their sins. Therefore, some Free Grace advocates have told them that they were already saved. Forever. And that is all they needed to hear. Now they can't be bothered to go near a church. If a Free Grace pastor warns them that they are going to lose heavenly reward, and that they are "not living up to who they truly are," they will just reason that everybody is going to

69. On a video included on the home page of the GES website (https://faithalone.org/), Robert Wilkin, the Executive Director of GES, specifically states that Free Grace proponents do not believe in perseverance (accessed December 27, 2024). Likewise, one of the affirmations of the FGA (https://www.freegracealliance.com/about-us/) states, "Spiritual growth . . . is not necessarily manifested uniformly in every believer" (accessed December 27, 2024).

> be happy in heaven anyway, so why care? And they persist in their lives of sin. And they are lost.[70]

Third, assurance is a gift of God's grace based on the unbreakable promises of God's Word. But we should likewise be aware of the subjective aspects of assurance: perseverance in good works and the internal testimony of the Holy Spirit. The stool of assurance rests on all three of these legs. Indeed, the promises of God are primary and strongest, but the other two are valuable and biblical, as the Second London Baptist Confession reminds us.[71]

And finally, if the readers of this book happen to live in a place apart from Free Grace teaching, they should ask themselves why assurance is not discussed all that often. In that part of the evangelical world where Reformed theology dominates, Carson surmises that popular eschatology has become so this-worldly that there are "very little futurist elements left, except at the merely creedal level." He continues, "If we do not long for the consummation of our salvation in the new heaven and the new earth, for the *visio Dei* that is the believer's inheritance, then there is little point in talking about our assurance of gaining it."[72] But what about readers who may have frequent contact with Free Grace theology and who hear about assurance all the time? Are they looking not only at the promises of God but also at their perseverance and the testimony of the Spirit to their place in God's family? We can thank the Free Grace teachers for reminding us of the important truth of assurance, even as we look to Christ for his aid in completing the good work he has begun in us and so persevere in faith and good works to the end.

FREE GRACE THEOLOGY AND ANTINOMIANISM

As mentioned in chapter 1, imbalance in teaching about sanctification often results in negative and sometimes erroneous teaching for Christians. I believe that Free Grace theology's emphasis on assurance has sadly eclipsed a more biblically informed perspective on perseverance and consequently falls under the umbrella of antinomianism. If we recall the six characteristics of antinomian teaching gleaned from

---

70. Grudem, *"Free Grace" Theology*, 78.
71. Second London Baptist Confession 18.2.
72. Carson, "Reflections," 7.

our study of the history of this error in chapter 6, we find two ways in which Free Grace teaching intersects with antinomianism. First, Free Grace proponents hold that obedience cannot be used as a basis of assurance (characteristic 5); this point is trumpeted on both websites and in all Free Grace written material. Second, Free Grace teachers misunderstand the relationship between justification and sanctification by failing to acknowledge the obedient fruit of sanctification that necessarily issues from justification and in this way create too strong a barrier between the two (characteristic 4). When Free Grace teachers minimize the importance of repentance, claim that believers can fall away, and prioritize positional truth, they allow for lawless living—for antinomianism.

CHAPTER 8

RADICAL GRACE AND PERSEVERANCE

As we continue our journey down the antinomian river, we have considered the origins and characteristics of antinomianism as we studied its history in chapter 6. Floating into the current portion of the river, we have noticed that it has widened a bit due to the confluence of three tributaries of antinomian teaching. In chapter 7 we learned about the first of these streams—Free Grace theology—whose source is the Chaferian model of sanctification. Now in chapter 8 we come to the next stream, Radical Grace.[1] Unlike Free Grace, Radical Grace has its point of origin in the Reformed model of sanctification. The third tributary—Hyper-Grace—is the focus of chapter 9.

These three streams of antinomian teaching have precipitated a perilous departure from the NT's demands for obedience in the life of the Christian and therefore from the commands to persevere in the faith. So how does Radical Grace teaching intersect with perseverance and antinomianism? I answer this question by first considering the naming of this Reformed-based grace teaching.[2] Second, I look at the history and proponents of this teaching. Third, I investigate the doctrinal teaching of Radical Grace. Fourth, I evaluate how Radical Grace doctrine meshes with the NT theology of perseverance. And finally, I compare the tenets of Radical Grace teaching to those of antinomianism in order to see if it deserves inclusion in the club of erroneous distorters of perseverance.

---

1. Portions of this chapter were first published as Jon Pratt, "Radical Grace," *GDJT* 1 (2022): 85–109. https://g3min.org/library-resources/gloria-deo-journal-of-theology-1/. Used with permission.
2. Unlike Free Grace and Hyper-Grace, this group is still in its formative stages and has no identifying name.

RADICAL GRACE: THE NAME

At the outset we encounter the challenge of naming this group.[3] Since this group has been speaking and writing about their focus for less than fifteen years, neither its proponents nor its opponents have yet to develop an official name for it. Indeed, Zane Hodges had been writing and speaking about Free Grace for at least fifteen years prior to the establishment of the Grace Evangelical Society, so it should not surprise us that the group I am about to discuss does not have a clear identity, a clear leader, or any particularly clear doctrinal statement. Furthermore, the broad range of denominational representatives who write and speak about this subject mean that an identifying name is unlikely to be forthcoming.

However, several have attempted to label this teaching. Perhaps Jen Wilkin's suggestion of "celebratory failurism" is a bit too pejorative.[4] Gerhard Forde proposed "radical Lutheranism," but this is a bit too narrow, considering the significant number of non-Lutherans who fit under this group's umbrella.[5] Another option is "confessionalism," offered by a group called Theocast, but it is too general to be helpful.[6]

Lacking any particularly appropriate name, I have labeled this group Radical Grace. Like the Free Grace and Hyper-Grace teachers, Radical Grace proponents emphasize the importance of grace in the lives of believers. What distinguishes Radical Grace from these other grace groups is the agreement of its adherents to the law-gospel distinction

---

3. I was first apprised of this group through a presentation by Gary Gilley at the national IFCA conference in South Bend, IN (June 2018). He used the phrase "Liberate Theology" to describe the group, based upon the Liberate Conference that was hosted by Tullian Tchividjian and held in Fort Lauderdale, FL, from 2012–2015. Since the Liberate Network was dissolved in 2017, I think a different name would better describe the group. See https://tottministries.org/sanctification-debates-part-1/ and his three-part series of articles: "Sanctification Debates: Parts 1–3," *Think on These Things* 24.1–3 (Jan–June 2018).
4. Jen Wilkin, "Failure Is Not a Virtue," The Gospel Coalition, May 1, 2014, https://www.thegospelcoalition.org/article/failure-is-not-a-virtue/.
5. Gerhard O. Forde, *A More Radical Gospel: Essays on Eschatology, Authority, Atonement, and Ecumenism*, ed. Mark C. Mattes and Steven D. Paulson (Grand Rapids: Eerdmans, 2004), 7, writes: "My thesis is that Lutherans . . . should become even more radical proponents of the tradition that gave them birth and has brought them thus far. . . . Let us be radicals: not conservatives or liberals, fundagelicals or charismatics (or whatever other brand of something-less-than gospel entices), but radicals: radical preachers and practitioners of the gospel by justification by faith without the deeds of the law."
6. Jon Moffitt, Justin Perdue, and Jeremy Buehler, *Faith vs Faithfulness: A Primer on Rest* (Theocast, 2019), 4–5. This is a slightly revised version of Ryan Haskins et al., *A Primer on Pietism: Its Characteristics and Inevitable Impact on the Christian Life* (pub. by author, 2017), 11. Also see Ryan Haskins et al., *A Pilgrim's Guide to Rest* (pub. by author, 2018), 8.

first emphasized by Martin Luther and how they equate the concepts of gospel and grace as a way of describing the NT teaching about the Christian life. Thus, law is anything that makes demands on sinners in that it gives imperatives that condemn. On the other hand, gospel makes no demands because it "comes in the indicative voice" and issues in unconditional grace.[7] This context of grace, then, best explains the emphasis of Radical Grace teachers in contrast to a law-oriented moralism that stifles freedom and enhances guilt-ridden legalism.

In using the modifier *radical* to qualify this group of grace teachers, I am giving a nod to Gerhard Forde, who called his approach to the Christian life "Radical Lutheranism."[8] But I am not going to describe this group as Lutheran, for its advocates hail from several Protestant traditions.[9]

Now that we have settled the question of nomenclature, we move next to the history of Radical Grace.

RADICAL GRACE: THE HISTORY AND PROPONENTS

Protestant Environment of Radical Grace

Of the many theological challenges confronting the reformers in the sixteenth century, the distinction between law and gospel as it relates to

7. William McDavid, Ethan Richardson, and David Zahl, *Law and Gospel: A Theology for Sinners (and Saints)* (Charlottesville, VA: Mockingbird Ministries, 2015), 48–52.
8. Gerhard Forde, "Radical Lutheranism," *LQ* 1 (1987): 5–18. Most, if not all, of the Radical Grace advocates rely on Forde's writings whether or not they specifically cite him. His influence should not be underestimated. Not only is his use of "radical" to describe his theology of sanctification in Lutheranism of unique historical import but also is his advocacy of the theology of the cross as opposed to the theology of glory. See Gerhard Forde, *On Being a Theologian of the Cross: Reflections on Luther's Heidelberg Disputation, 1518* (Grand Rapids: Eerdmans, 1997). Mickey L. Mattox, review of *On Being a Theologian of the Cross: Reflections on Luther's Heidelberg Disputation, 1518* by Gerhard Forde, *JETS* 42.3 (1999): 537, aptly describes Forde's theology of the cross:

   > Forde . . . lays out in clearest terms Luther's understanding of the wondrous promises of the Gospel. Only when God has become our most relentless enemy and truly slain us with the Law does he raise us up to new life by means of the Word. In both cases . . . it is God who takes the initiative; the sinner suffers both the condemnation of the Law and the promise of the Gospel as realities given from without. In this sense, one can speak of being a theologian of the cross only as one created by God, and not of becoming one as if it could be done through the exercise of some innate human capacity. . . . This knowledge in turn enables the Christian to distinguish between theologies of glory and the theology of the cross.

9. These include Lutherans, Presbyterians, Anglicans, Baptists, and nondenominationalists.

the doctrine of justification was certainly near the top of the list.[10] On the one hand, the Reformers taught that the law could never save but rather served to make demands that could never be met; law corresponds to the effort of doing good works as a way of gaining favor with God, something that could never occur because justification can never be attained by works (Rom 3:28; Gal 2:16; Eph 2:8–9). On the other hand, the gospel speaks of the free gift of grace given to the sinner by faith. There is absolutely no effort or good works that are required for justification because Christ's righteousness is imputed to the ungodly as a gift (Rom 3:24–26).[11]

Thus, we should never mix law and gospel when calling a sinner to repentance. The unbeliever can receive justification by faith alone (gospel) apart from any works (law). Every evangelical believer affirms this truth of keeping law and gospel separate when speaking of our justification. But how do these two ideas relate to the believer's progressive sanctification? Does the law have any connection to the gospel when speaking of the believer's growth in holiness *after* her justification? Indeed, if the Reformers believed that the law says *do* while the gospel says *done*, then how do these two concepts relate to the numerous imperatives found in the New Testament? While Luther and Calvin differed a bit in how they articulated the place of law in the believer's life, they agreed that obedience to the moral law was necessary. The WCF 19.6 clearly affirms, "Although true believers be not under the law, as a covenant of works, to be thereby justified, or condemned; yet is it of great use to them, as well as to others; in that, as a rule of life informing them of the will of God, and their duty, it directs and binds them to walk accordingly." Calvin referred to this function of the law as its "third use."[12] And so a basic tenet of

10. Lutheran and Reformed theologians convened at the Marburg Colloquy in 1529 and agreed on fourteen articles of faith. Of these, "articles 4 through 7 all implicitly employ the distinction between law and gospel as a criterion by which Christ *alone* is identified as the subject of God's saving grace" (Jonathan A. Linebaugh, "Introduction," in *God's Two Words: Law and Gospel in the Lutheran and Reformed Traditions*, ed. Jonathan A. Linebaugh [Grand Rapids: Eerdmans, 2018], 2). See Martin Luther, *Luther's Works,* ed. and trans. Martin E. Lehmann, 55 vols. (Philadelphia: Fortress Press, 1971), 38:85–89, for the presentation of these articles and the significant reformers who signed their agreement including Luther, Melanchthon, Zwingli, Bucer, Oecolampadius, and Agricola.

11. Myron Houghton, *Law and Grace* (Schaumburg, IL: Regular Baptist Press, 2011), 9, explains this distinction well: "The law makes demands while the gospel does not make any demands. In other words, the law says *do*, while the gospel says *done*" (emphasis original).

12. John Calvin, *Institutes of the Christian Religion*, ed. John T. McNeill, trans. Ford Lewis Battles, 2 vols.(Philadelphia: Westminster, 1960), 2.7.12, "The third and principal use [of

the Reformers is an explanation and endorsement of how the moral law (the ceremonial and civil aspects of the law are abrogated with the coming of Christ) ought to function as a "means of sanctification" for believers.[13]

Since this connection of law and gospel in relation to sanctification is so readily affirmed by Protestants, we can understand how people growing up in circles where the third use of the law is taught could easily slip into a form of merit-based performance in their efforts to grow in sanctification.[14] And it is the desire to correct this faulty practice that has generated the existence and development of its opposing but equally as errant nemesis, Radical Grace.

Antecedent Influences on Radical Grace

Three antecedent influences stand behind the current form of Radical Grace. First, we have "Radical Lutheranism," particularly indebted to theologian Gerhard Forde (1927–2005), who coined the phrase.[15] Interestingly, Forde decried historical antinomianism, but it appears that some of his provocative comments about sanctification (e.g., "Sanctification is a matter of being grasped by the unconditional grace of God and having now to live in that light. It is a matter of getting used to our justification"[16]) have served as fodder for

the law], which pertains more closely to the proper purpose of the law, finds its place among believers in whose hearts the Spirit of God already lives and reigns." Lutheran scholars have debated whether or not Luther held to the third use of the law. Edward A. Englebrecht, "Luther's Threefold Use of the Law," *CTQ* 75 (2011): 135–50, argued that Luther held to the third use of the law as seen in a Christmas sermon (1522) and in a lecture on 1 Tim 1:8–9 (1528). But Gerhard Forde, *Christ and the Christian Life* (Minneapolis: Fortress, 1984), 208, argued that Luther did not. Also see Houghton, *Law and Grace*, 10; and Jones, *Antinomianism*, 3–5.

13. Sinclair Ferguson, "The Reformed View," in Alexander, *Christian Spirituality*, 68–71. Similarly, we see the same kind of treatment of Calvin's third use of the law in two other "five views" books: Anthony A. Hoekema, "The Reformed Perspective," in Dieter, *Five Views on Sanctification*, 59–90; and Willem A. VanGemeren, "The Law Is the Perfection of Righteousness in Jesus Christ: A Reformed Perspective," in *The Law, the Gospel, and the Modern Christian: Five Views*, ed. Wayne Strickland (Grand Rapids: Zondervan Academic, 1993), 13–58.
14. There are likely several reasons why people might slip into merit-based performance besides an emphasis on the third use of the law. I am simply acknowledging that this basic plank in the Reformers' platform has contributed to merit-based performance for many.
15. Forde, "Radical Lutheranism," 5–18.
16. Gerhard O. Forde, "The Lutheran View," in Alexander, *Christian Spirituality*, 22–23. See also Forde, *Christ and the Christian Life*, 195, "Sanctification happens. The good works come out of spontaneity, the freedom, the '*hilaritas*' of faith."

Radical Grace.[17] Second, we have the Anglican influence of Paul Zahl and Robert Farrar Capon, both Episcopal priests, who emphasized the freeing power of grace to the detriment of the enslaving nature of the law.[18] Third, we have statements about grace and law from the Reformed confessions (e.g. Westminster Confession of Faith, London Baptist Confession, etc.), Luther and Calvin themselves, and modern Reformed scholars that are used to downplay the importance of obedience to the imperatives while emphasizing the significance of the indicatives.[19]

The Proponents and Writings of Radical Grace

Tullian Tchividjian exercised a huge influence in organizing support for Radical Grace. Tchividjian, the grandson of Billy Graham, took over as senior pastor at Coral Ridge Presbyterian, following D. James Kennedy. This move included a merger of churches as Tchividjian's church, New City Presbyterian, united with Coral Ridge in 2009. Between 2005 and 2015, Tchividjian published eight books, but the two that most reflected his views on grace in regard to sanctification were *Jesus + Nothing = Everything* (2011) and *One Way Love* (2013).[20] He also blogged regularly on The Gospel Coalition website until he was removed due to "an increasingly strident debate going on around the issue of sanctification."[21] Just prior to his removal,

17. Michael Allen, *Sanctification*, New Studies in Dogmatics (Grand Rapids: Zondervan Academic, 2017), 30n15, writes: "The Radical Lutheranism of Forde . . . has exercised wider influence at the popular level in recent years, connecting to a number of Presbyterian or Reformed ministries (e.g., Tullian Tchividjian), to so-called reformational Anglican circles (e.g., Mockingbird), and elsewhere."
18. Paul F. M. Zahl, *Grace in Practice: A Theology of Everyday Life* (Grand Rapids: Eerdmans, 2007), 26–41; Paul F. M. Zahl, *Who Will Deliver Us? The Present Power of the Death of Christ* (1983; repr., Eugene, OR: Wipf & Stock, 2008); and Robert Farrar Capon, *Kingdom, Grace, Judgment: Paradox, Outrage, and Vindication in the Parables of Jesus* (Grand Rapids: Eerdmans, 2002).
19. Moffitt, Perdue, and Buehler, *Faith vs Faithfulness*, 4, state: "We do look back to the confessions of faith that were produced during the era of the Reformation. These confessions arose, as confessions typically do, because theological clarity was required. The Reformation was a response to the rampant moralism and works-based system of the medieval church. Therefore, the confessions that were produced out of it push back against moralism."
20. Tullian Tchividjian, *Jesus + Nothing = Everything* (Wheaton, IL: Crossway, 2011); and Tullian Tchividjian, *One Way Love* (Colorado Springs: David C. Cook, 2013).
21. Don Carson, "On Some Recent Changes at TGC," The Gospel Coalition, May 21, 2014, https://www.thegospelcoalition.org/article/on-some-recent-changes-at-tgc/. Carson also stated, "The differences were doctrinal and probably even more matters of pastoral practice and wisdom."

Tchividjian and Kevin DeYoung had engaged in a spirited exchange over the matter of sanctification we are considering in this chapter.[22] Tchividjian also hosted an annual conference at his church from 2012–2015 entitled "Liberate." Speakers included Steve Brown, Matt Chandler, Elyse Fitzpatrick, Ray Ortlund, Paul Tripp, Michael Horton, and Bryan Chapell. The conference led to the formation of the Liberate network, which would likely have grown into an organization similar to 9Marks, The Gospel Coalition, or the Grace Evangelical Society.

While Tchividjian was certainly the most familiar face of Radical Grace from 2011–2015, there were certainly others who advocated the same theological ideas and who continue to do so. Theocast began in 2015 when a group of four pastors from the Nashville area (Byron Yawn, Ryan Haskins, Jeremy Litts, and Jon Moffitt, who called themselves "The Boys") started a podcast and eventually published two books trumpeting Radical Grace ideas: *A Primer on Pietism: Its Characteristics and Inevitable Impact on the Christian Life* (2017) and *A Pilgrim's Guide to Rest* (2018).[23] They also produced a weekly podcast from December 2015–June 2019 dealing with subjects like sanctification, assurance, law and gospel, Reformed theology, and "Pietism."[24] These and other resources were available through their website.[25] Jon Moffitt took over the website in 2019 and continues to serve as the director.[26] Joining Moffitt in 2019 were Justin Perdue and

22. While all blogposts of Tullian Tchividjian have been removed from the TGC website, DeYoung's are still accessible. See this blogpost, which gives some background to the situation: Kevin DeYoung, "What We All Agree on, What We (Probably) Don't, in This Sanctification Debate," The Gospel Coalition, May 13, 2014, https://www.thegospelcoalition.org/blogs/kevin-deyoung/what-we-all-agree-on-and-what-we-probably-dont-in-this-sanctification-debate/.
23. See n6. Both books were jointly authored by all four men and published by Theocast. Both are now out of print, though they can still be purchased on Amazon.
24. Pietism, according to The Boys, is synonymous with moralism or legalism; it is preoccupied with the interior of the Christian life; its main focus is on the *duty* of the Christian above all other realities; it believes that *obligation* precedes *assurance*; and it is heavy on the imperatives of Scripture. All these phrases come from Haskins et al., *Primer on Pietism*, 8–17. In the updated revision, Moffitt, Perdue, and Buehler, *Faith vs Faithfulness*, 1–3, pietism is described as "an overemphasis on the life of the Christian and what the Christian should be doing" and an "obsession with ongoing improvement."
25. See https://theocast.org/ (accessed January 5, 2025).
26. Moffitt also serves as the pastor of Grace Reformed Church in Spring Hill, TN, https://theocast.org/about/, accessed December 28, 2024.

Jimmy Buehler,[27] and for the next two years all three collaborated on the weekly podcast and the writing of two books: *Faith vs Faithfulness: A Primer on Rest* and *Safe in Christ: A Primer on Assurance*.[28] Then in 2021, Buehler stepped away and Moffitt and Perdue have continued to offer the weekly podcast along with blogposts and other biblical materials.

Another strain of Radical Grace teaching can be found at the website Trueface.[29] This organization is led by John Lynch, Bruce McNicol, and Bill Thrall. These three have collaborated on Trueface's most important book, *The Cure*.[30] While Trueface is not as theologically oriented as Liberate or Theocast, the group similarly emphasizes God's grace and acceptance while denigrating the kind of moralism that tempts Christians to keep striving to please God.

Three organizations, each of which provides written resources (blogs and books), podcasts, and national and regional conferences, strongly emphasize Radical Grace theology. Note the mission statements of each.

- 1517.org: "To declare and defend the Good News that you are forgiven and free on account of Christ alone."[31]
- Mockingbird: "Nothing else in the world matters but the kindness of grace, God's gift to the suffering."[32]
- Lark: "We believe Jesus set us free to stop striving and start living in the *freedom* faith was always meant to bring."[33]

Likewise, the site 1517.org has few qualms in admitting its Lutheran roots and connection to Forde's radical Lutheranism.[34] The staff and

27. Justin Perdue pastors Covenant Baptist Church in Asheville, NC, and Jimmy Buehler formerly pastored Christ Community Church in Willmar, MN.
28. Moffitt, Perdue, and Buehler, *Faith vs Faithfulness*; this is an updated revision of *A Primer on Pietism* (pub. by author, 2017). Also see Moffitt, Perdue, and Buehler, *Safe in Christ*.
29. See https://www.trueface.org/, accessed January 5, 2025.
30. John Lynch, Bruce McNicol, and Bill Thrall, *The Cure* (Phoenix, AZ: Trueface, 2011). A lot of the concepts found in this book first appeared in Bill Thrall, Bruce McNicol, and John Lynch, *TrueFaced* (Colorado Springs: NavPress, 2004).
31. See https://www.1517.org/about, accessed December 28, 2024.
32. See https://mbird.com/about/history-and-mission/, accessed December 28, 2024.
33. See https://larksite.com/, accessed December 28, 2024.
34. See https://www.1517.org/, accessed January 5, 2025. On a personal note, I attended a 1517.org regional conference in Burnsville, MN, in 2019. I was intrigued by a sticker on Scott Keith's laptop, which he clearly displayed during his speaking session: "Forde Lives." Gerhard Forde died in 2005!

scholars associated with 1517.org include Scott Keith, Chad Bird, Steven Paulson, Paul Hillman, and Daniel Van Voorhis.[35]

Mockingbird claims to have no formal denominational affiliation, but its founder David Zahl serves on the staff of an Episcopal church and the website features a podcast with David and his two brothers, John and Simeon, who are the sons of Paul Zahl, an Episcopal priest.[36] Furthermore, of the thirty books for sale on the site, half are written by one of the Zahls or Robert Capon, another Episcopal priest. The signature book of the website is *Law and Gospel*, which clearly demonstrates the main themes of Radical Grace, which will be delineated below.[37]

Lark was founded by Russ Johnson in 2014 and originally was called The Table Network before changing its name in 2021.[38] Shortly after its founding, Tony Sorci joined Johnson, and they have labored together, creating a network of fellowships. Under the Table Network label, they published *Slow Down*.[39] Many of the same Radical Grace ideas from that book are found in their newest Lark publication, *Reclaim*.[40]

---

35. Recently, 1517.org lost two of its major fellows: Rod Rosenbladt (1942–2024) and John Warwick Montgomery (1931–2024), both of whom had contributed many titles to the booklist on the website. The booklist also includes many titles by Chad Bird; in regard to Radical Grace see Chad Bird, *Upside-Down Spirituality: The 9 Essential Failures of a Faithful Life* (Grand Rapids: Baker Academic, 2019), and Chad Bird, *Your God Is Too Glorious: Finding God in the Most Unexpected Places* (Grand Rapids: Baker Academic, 2018).

    Steven Paulson, who is a senior scholar-in-residence at 1517, is the clear frontrunner among Lutherans who are promoting and building upon Forde's radical Lutheranism. See Steven D. Paulson, *Luther's Outlaw God*, 3 vols. (Minneapolis: Augsburg Fortress, 2018–2021). While his three volumes do not necessarily deal with Radical Grace directly (and certainly not in a popular way), they share all the qualities of Forde's project, including his distinction between law and grace, his denial of the third use of the law, and his theology of the cross. For a critique of Forde's theology of the cross see Christopher D. Jackson, "Luther's Theologian of the Cross and Theologian of Glory Distinction Reconsidered," *ProEccl* 29 (2020): 336–51; and for a critique of Forde's view of the law see Jack Kilcrease, "Gerhard Forde's Doctrine of the Law: A Confessional Lutheran Critique," *CTQ* 75 (2011): 151–79; and Engelbrecht, "Luther's Threefold Use of the Law," 135–50.
36. See https://mbird.com/, accessed January 5, 2025.
37. McDavid, Richardson, and Zahl, *Law and Gospel*.
38. Lark is the general name of this nonprofit organization, which describes itself thusly: "We create space for unhurried conversations and offer undiluted resources to help people live in the freedom faith was always meant to bring" (https://larksite.com/, accessed December 28, 2024).
39. Russ Johnson, Gino Curcuruto, and Tony Sorci, *Slow Down* (Bellevue, WA: Missional Challenge, 2017). This book is still available on Amazon but is no longer on the website.
40. Russ Johnson and Tony Sorci, *Reclaim* (Coppell, TX: Lark, 2021). It is difficult to determine the denominational connections of Lark. This book cites Anglican, Presbyterian, and Lutheran sources, yet it seems to lean in a post-emergent-church direction (e.g.,

RADICAL GRACE: THE DOCTRINE

As we discuss the teaching of Radical Grace, remember that Radical Grace does not promote heresy and that it is within the boundaries of orthodoxy. In fact, it points out a key problem in the lives of many Christians today—moralistic/legalistic, performance-based approaches to sanctification. Radical Grace teaches that Christians do not gain more of God's love through obedience and performance, and it reminds us that our security in Christ and assurance of salvation can never be lost despite the sins we commit after our justification.[41] Their reminders of the meaning and application of God's grace are refreshing and convicting because it is so easy to stumble (even if absentmindedly) into the ditch of self-sufficiency and self-improvement in one's personal walk with Christ. Additionally, Radical Grace's emphasis on the acceptance of believers by Christ apart from any moral standard but the imputed righteousness of Christ gives freedom to those bound by "pleasing man" issues on the one hand and encouragement to those burdened with insecurity and fear on the other.

Nonetheless, imbalance in teaching always has negative consequences, and I fear that unguarded statements and overly triumphant perspectives have resulted in a harmful deemphasis of the imperatives of the NT. This defines the basic problem at issue: Radical Grace has plunged so deeply into the indicative ditch of sanctification that their followers are finding it difficult to see, much less embrace, the importance of the imperatives on the other side of the road.

What Is the Problem?

In treating the teaching of Radical Grace I will first consider the problem it is seeking to address and then discuss the solution its proponents offer to that problem. First, what is the problem? Though all these authors agree on the problem, they tend to use different terms and descriptions to define it. For Johnson and Sorci, it is "moralism" taught by the "Church[, which is] a place of performance and challenge" and emphasizes "personal morality."[42] For another Radical Grace teacher

---

"Providing people with a place to belong on their way to belief" [112]), all the while trumpeting "reckless" (57, 119) and "indiscriminate" (81, 85, 96) grace.

41. Gary Gilley, "Sanctification Debates, Part 1," Tottministries.org, https://tottministries.org/sanctification-debates-part-1/.

42. Johnson and Sorci, *Reclaim*, 20, 42.

the problem is "reading texts that *are not commandments* as though they are" and turning them into "moralistic teaching."[43] Theocast refers to this problem as "Pietism." The authors of *Faith vs. Faithfulness* seek to describe the term by providing eleven characteristics of a pietistic religious context. Here are a few from the list:

1. "the gospel is viewed as an entry point to the Christian life" and "is often a kind of a footnote in the corporate gathering";
2. "law and gospel are often mixed";
3. "the motivation to press on in the Christian life . . . is often doubt, fear, and worry"; and
4. "the emphasis is almost exclusively on personal spiritual disciplines as the means of spiritual growth."[44]

The authors of *The Cure* use an allegory to compare the two different ways that Christians approach their walk with God. They either live in the Room of Grace or in the Room of Good Intentions; it is problematic to live in the second room. Those in the Room of Good Intentions live by the two mottos hanging on the wall in the room: "Striving hard to be all God wants me to be" and "Working on my sin to achieve an intimate relationship with God." We can summarize this with the formula "More right behavior + Less wrong behavior = Godliness."[45]

McDavid, Richardson, and Zahl call the problem "misguided Semipelagianism," which means that "God saves us and then the work of moral progress is up to us."[46] In another book David Zahl labels this semi-pelagianism as "high anthropology," which he describes as attributing too much moral ability to the sinner.[47]

Finally, Tchividjian uses "legalism, performancism, and moralism," but he tends to use "performancism" most frequently. He explains that performancism "happens when *what we need to do,* not what Jesus

43. R. W. Glenn, *Crucifying Morality: The Gospel of the Beatitudes* (Wapwallopen, PA: Shepherd Press, 2013), 17–18 (emphasis original).
44. Moffitt, Perdue, and Buehler, *Faith vs Faithfulness*, 6–9.
45. Lynch, McNicol, and Thrall, *The Cure*, 14–17.
46. McDavid, Richardson, and Zahl, *Law and Gospel*, 68.
47. David Zahl, *Low Anthropology: The Unlikely Key to a Gracious View of Others (and Yourself)* (Grand Rapids: Brazos, 2022), 27, describes high anthropology as perfectionism, the idea that human beings can continue to get a lot closer to being perfect than they are right now.

has already done, becomes the end game." This attitude demonstrates itself in moralistic living and preaching. Concerning living, the moralist believes that his "good behavior is required to *keep* God's favor." Regarding preaching, moralistic sermons "provide nothing more than a 'to do' list, strengthening our bondage to a performance-driven approach to the Christian life. It's all law (what we must do) and no gospel (what Jesus has done)."[48] Three results occur when performancism is one's manner of approach to the Christian life: (1) we turn into complainers like the older brother in the parable of the prodigal son, (2) it obscures the goodness of the good news because most lost people think that doing good works saves them, and (3) it traps us in slavery and despair.[49]

Thus, the problem for Christians according to Radical Grace is that, even though believers have been justified by faith apart from works, they have slipped into a works-based approach to their sanctification, believing that their effort in doing good works will gain them greater favor with God.[50] In other words, these moralistic, performance-based, Semipelagian Christians have fallen into the legalistic ditch of the sanctification road. This leads us to see how Radical Grace teachers believe that this problem can be solved.

What Is the Solution?

The second step in our discussion of Radical Grace is to learn how these teachers believe that the problem of legalism should be resolved. In basic terms, Radical Grace teaches that believers must believe in and rest upon the indicatives of our salvation. We can summarize their approach to the solution under five broad ideas:

1. Relax and rest! "The bottom line is this, Christian: because of Christ's work on your behalf, God doesn't dwell on your sin the way you do. So, relax . . . and you'll actually start to get better."[51]

48. Tchividjian, *Jesus + Nothing*, 46–49 (emphases original). Also see McDavid, Richardson, and Zahl, *Law and Gospel*, 61: "'Performancism' is a helpful way to describe what it looks like to justify ourselves."
49. Tchividjian, *Jesus + Nothing*, 52–54.
50. For Forde, *Christ and the Christian Life*, 207–211, Christians who hold to the third use of the law have done just this—they have slipped into a works-based sanctification. Zahl, *Low Anthropology*, 194, also opposes the third use of the law: "A religion of low anthropology does not recalibrate the law of God or propagate rumors about the human ability to fulfill it."
51. Tchividjian, *Jesus + Nothing*, 184.

"The believer rests in the Father's arms instead of laboring to climb into them. We rest knowing our status is forever fixed."[52] "Christianity is about coming over and over again to rest in the life that Jesus lived and the death that he died for you as a gift of sheer grace."[53]

2. Remember and remind yourself! "Remembering, revisiting, and rediscovering the reality of our justification every day is the hard work we're called to do if we're going to grow."[54] "If you continually remind yourself that you are accepted completely and solely because of the comprehensively perfect righteousness of Christ, then you can be confident that he will never reject you."[55]
3. Trust in God and believe the gospel! "At the core, we're just learning to trust and depend on our new identity. We're learning to live out of who God says we are on our worst day. So a statement like 'It's less important that anything gets fixed, but that nothing is hidden' is an example of living out of our new identity."[56] "Real spiritual progress happens when our typical, natural understanding of progress is rooted out. The key to Christian growth, then, is not first behaving better; it's believing better—believing more deeply what Jesus has already accomplished."[57]
4. Receive Christ's work on your behalf! Using Christ's instruction about children, Johnson and Sorci say that children "are the quintessential models of reception. This example is fitting when you realize that Christ's Kingdom is all about God giving and us receiving, not us accomplishing."[58] "Only Christians know that the thing they so desperately need is the righteousness of Jesus, and they want to receive that gift anew every day."[59]

---

52. Haskins et al., *Primer on Pietism*, 25.
53. Glenn, *Crucifying Morality*, 19.
54. Tchividjian, "Work Hard! But in Which Direction?" The Gospel Coalition, June 8, 2011. See https://theaquilareport.com/the-role-of-effort-in-sanctification-a-dialogue-between-kevin-deyoung-and-tullian-tchividjian/100/. I thank Bryan Blazosky for helping to locate this exchange between Tchividjian and DeYoung.
55. Glenn, *Crucifying Morality*, 64.
56. Lynch, McNicol, and Thrall, *The Cure*, 84.
57. Tchividjian, *Jesus + Nothing*, 172–73.
58. Johnson and Sorci, *Reclaim*, 87.
59. Glenn, *Crucifying Morality*, 64.

5. Grow in understanding the gospel! "Whatever sanctification includes, it begins with an understanding of who we are in Christ and what He has freed us from."[60] "The righteousness that Jesus [gives] . . . is the righteousness that you begin to possess as you grow in your understanding of what Jesus has done for you."[61]

These same five themes—relax, remember, trust, receive, and grow in understanding—are found again and again in Radical Grace literature. I have limited each of the five categories to a few quotes for each, and I could have given many more. For example, note these provocative statements quite common among these writers:

- "*Application* is almost always a code word for *law.*"[62]
- Jesus meets the Christian: "He puts His hands on my shoulders, staring into my eyes. No disappointment. No condemnation. Only delight. Only love. He pulls me into a bear hug, so tight it knocks the breath out of me for a moment. . . . After several moments, with a straight face He says, 'That is a lot of sin. A whole lot of sin. Don't you ever sleep?' He starts laughing, and I start laughing."[63]
- "Sanctification is more about not having to do what we did before and less about avoiding bad things we once did. . . . Paul never offers sanctification as the measuring stick of God's pleasure toward us."[64]
- "Jesus I can love. He does everything, I do nothing; I trust him. It is a nifty arrangement."[65]
- "We are not expected to be doers of God's command, but believers in God's promise."[66]
- "God works *his* work in *you,* which is the work already accomplished by Christ. Our hard work, therefore, means coming to a greater understanding of *his* work."[67]

---

60. Haskins et al., *A Pilgrim's Guide to Rest*, 125.
61. Glenn, *Crucifying Morality*, 105.
62. Tchividjian, *One Way Love*, 155 (emphasis original).
63. Lynch, McNicol, and Thrall, *The Cure*, 22.
64. Haskins et al., *Pilgrim's Guide to Rest*, 125.
65. Capon, *Parables of Grace*, 98.
66. Donavon Riley, "God Commands the Impossible and That's Good," March 7, 2018, https://1517.org/articles/god-commands-the-impossible-and-thats-good.
67. Tchividjian, *Jesus + Nothing*, 96 (emphasis original).

- "Good works are more a matter of the left hand not knowing what the right hand is doing. . . . Sanctification tends to feel more like losing than accruing, of getting smaller rather than larger."[68]

The discerning reader may observe that this language sounds very similar to Keswick's idea of "let go and let God."[69] The quietism displayed in each of these instances, however, is based upon different interests. For Keswick theology, letting go and letting God was the description of the crisis experience one needs to have in order to enter into the spiritual realm and out of the carnal realm; it is the ticket to the *beginning* of growth.[70] For Radical Grace, relaxing, receiving, and so on are behaviors that wise Christians engage in as they grow in their maturity. Since the Reformed model of sanctification assumes an inevitable connection between one's justification and sanctification, growth has already begun when faith is first exercised.[71] The quietism enjoined by Radical Grace teachers merely helps (in their thinking) to increase the growth trajectory more rapidly and to ensure that growth occurs with the proper biblical motivation.

RADICAL GRACE: ITS CONNECTION WITH PERSEVERANCE

As stated above, there are aspects of this teaching that, when in balance, can encourage Bible-loving Christians. We would be wise to ponder whether or not we give tacit approval to law-based, legalistic teaching that makes Christian living little more than rule following for the approval of God and others on the one hand or simplistic self-help lists of "be better Christians" on the other (e.g., "Five Principles for Christian Weight Loss" or "Eight Ways to Be a Better Friend"). Just as we are naturally inclined to think we can earn salvation—even for the justified sinner who has come to accept the gift of faith and who has been saved by grace alone apart from works (Eph 2:8–9)—we are tempted to slip into moralistic thinking when it comes to our sanctification. But I believe we are correct to raise a red flag of warning with regard to the emphases of Radical Grace as it has developed into its current form.

68. Zahl, *Low Anthropology*, 191.
69. Naselli, *No Quick Fix*.
70. Naselli, *No Quick Fix*, 30–39.
71. See the discussion of the Reformed model in chapter 1 and Jonathan R. Pratt, "Relationship between Justification and Spiritual Fruit," 162–78.

We do have a duty (and I use this word intentionally!) to guard the biblical doctrine of sanctification from those who would slip into imbalanced approaches. Sanctification is a work wrought by God with the willing involvement of the believer. This wonderful synergism results in the production of spiritual fruit in the believer's life as he responds to the Spirit's prompting work that enables him to do so. This is the mystery of sanctification so clearly stated by Paul in 1 Corinthians 15:10: "But by the grace of God I am what I am, and his grace toward me was not in vain. On the contrary, I worked harder than any of them, though it was not I, but the grace of God that is with me." We also see it displayed in Philippians 2:12–13: "Therefore, my beloved, as you have always obeyed, so now, not only as in my presence but much more in my absence, work out your own salvation with fear and trembling, for it is God who works in you, both to will and to work for his good pleasure."

Keeping the mystery of sanctification in mind, I now provide three ways Radical Grace deemphasizes the Christian's role in the sanctification process and in doing so minimizes the importance of the doctrine of perseverance, the truth that God will enable his children to produce good works to the end of their lives.

The Lack of Concern for Holiness

The first way Radical Grace teachers minimize perseverance is in their lack of concern for holiness. The "problem" of moralism/legalism/pietism seems overblown. Certainly there are believers among us who like rules and boundaries, coloring inside the lines, and clear lists. There are also pastors who focus on the externals in their sermons and in counseling, and who preach and teach in ways that reveal them to be shepherds insistent that their sheep stay in line. For people bound by or who lean toward a moralistic approach to the Christian life, Radical Grace reminds them that the indicatives of sanctification must not be forgotten in our walk of faith. But most would acknowledge that under the umbrella of conservative evangelical churches, the rule-keepers are in the minority. Too many believers in our churches live according to their feelings, like to color outside the lines, and do not like being told how they should live. It seems that the sanctification "problem" lies much more with *license* than with *legalism*. Many pastors are afraid to preach about holy living, fearing the backlash from their hearers; and as a result, our people are sometimes ignorant but probably more often happily guilt-free when it comes to making wise and discerning moral choices in their lives.[72]

The Lack of Concern for the Imperatives

The second way Radical Grace minimizes perseverance goes beyond the concern about holiness, expanding to the imperatives of sanctification as a whole. By relegating the imperatives to the realm of law and reminding believers that they now live in the grace and freedom of their justification, Radical Grace proponents diminish the importance of the imperatives while exalting the reality of the indicatives for the believer. This can have dangerous implications for the Christian, so much so that we will now take a short excursus on the imperatives of sanctification in order to see their necessity for the believer's perseverance.

We undertake this parenthesis in order to correct the overemphasis on the indicatives of sanctification so characteristic of Radical Grace because the best way to correct a distortion of the real thing is to understand the real thing better. Please understand that in looking more closely at the imperatives I do not want us to leap out of one ditch only to slide into the other. But so much of what is said in the Radical Grace literature either *ignores* these points about the imperatives or *caricatures* them. So please ponder with me the goal of the imperatives, the motivation for obeying the imperatives, and the effort required by the imperatives.[73]

---

72. Kevin DeYoung, *The Hole in Our Holiness* (Wheaton, IL: Crossway, 2012), 17–19, provides eight possible reasons why Christians are not apt to have a concern for holiness. (1) It was too common in the past to equate holiness with abstaining from a few taboo practices such as drinking, smoking, and dancing; godliness meant that you avoided the no-no list. (2) There is a fear that a passion for holiness makes you some kind of weird holdover from a bygone era. (3) Our churches have many unregenerate persons in them. (4) Our culture of cool regarding Christian freedom often means pushing the boundaries. (5) More progressive Christians think that labeling any behavior as "ungodly" is judgmental or intolerant (I recall hearing from a friend of mine who served as a principal in a Christian school being accused of "body-shaming" because she required the young ladies to wear modest dresses to the school-sponsored spring banquet). (6) If we are gospel-centered, we won't talk about imperatives or moral exertion; "We know legalism (salvation by law keeping) and antinomianism (salvation without the need for law keeping) are both wrong, but antinomianism feels like a much safer danger" (19). (7) Holiness is hard work, and who likes hard work? (8) Many Christians have given up on sanctification; since we're all hopeless sinners anyway, why bother?
73. This threefold outline comes from DeYoung, *Holiness*, 31–61, 79–91.

The Goal of the Imperatives: Holiness

If, indeed, God has called us to be holy as he is holy (1 Pet 1:15–16), then we need to consider what holiness looks like. First, holiness will involve conformation to and renewal in the image of Christ (Rom 8:29; 12:2; Gal 4:19; 2 Cor 3:18; 4:16; Phil 3:10). Second, it will be seen in a life marked by virtue rather than vice (Eph 4:25–5:3; Col 3:5–9; 12–15). Third, holiness is related to right thinking (Rom 12:3; 15:5; Phil 1:9–10; 4:8). Fourth, a holy life is marked by obedience to God's commands (John 14:23; 1 John 2:3). Finally, holiness shows itself in a clear conscience (Acts 24:16; Rom 14:23).

The Motivation for Obeying the Imperatives

One of the errors Radical Grace writers regularly point out is that performance-oriented Christians strive for holiness with wrong motives (e.g., pride, fear of judgment, desire to gain favor with God).[74] Although this caution is helpful, Scripture gives a multitude of proper motives, and we should consider the motives of rewards, God's love for us, and pleasing God.[75] First, the degree to which Christians obey corresponds with the rewards they will receive in glory.[76] This relates to the idea of different degrees of glory and happiness in eternity—glory will differ from saint to saint (1 Cor 3:14–15; 2 Cor 9:6: Lk 19:11–26).[77] Second, Mark Jones discusses the idea that the believer's obedience relates to the "complacent" love of God such that "the more we are like God, the more love we shall have from

74. Tchividjian, *Jesus + Nothing*, 46.

75. DeYoung, *Holiness*, 57–60, gives a list of forty proper motives with a corresponding verse or verses for each. He states, "As exhausting as this list might be, it could easily be doubled or tripled. God doesn't command obedience 'just cuz.' He gives us dozens of specific reasons to be holy."

76. Jones, *Antinomianism*, 71–76, provides a helpful discussion of this subject, using Edwards and Turretin as his primary resources.

77. Jonathan Edwards, *The Works of Jonathan Edwards*, rev. and corr. Edward Hickman, 2 vols. (London: Westley and Davis, 1834), 2:617: "There should be no reason why it should be a damp to the happiness of some in heaven that others are happier, than that their happiness should be damped by a bare possibility of greater happiness, supposing them to be all equal; for if they were all equal and all full of happiness, yet every one would know that greater happiness is possible, absolutely, and possible for them if God had but enlarged their capacity. And why should not they who are actuated by pure reason desire it, as much as if it were actually enjoyed by some beings?" Thanks to Bob Meredith for pointing me to this statement.

him."[78] Such verses as John 14:21–23, 15:10, and Jude 21 speak to the *increase* of God's love for his children in the "context of ongoing communion with God and Christ."[79] Third, while numerous Radical Grace quotes suggest that we can never please God by means of our post-conversion works, the NT makes it clear that we not only please God when we obey, but we are commanded to do so: "So whether we are at home or away, we make it our aim to please him" (2 Cor 5:9); "Finally, then, brothers, we ask and urge you in the Lord Jesus, that as you received from us how you ought to walk and to please God, just as you are doing, that you do so more and more" (1 Thess 4:1).[80] See also John 14:21; Romans 8:8–9; 14:18; Philippians 4:18; Colossians 1:10; 1 Thessalonians 2:4; 1 Timothy 2:3; 5:4; Hebrews 11:5–6; 13:16, 21; 1 John 3:22; Revelation 3:15–16.[81]

The Effort Required by the Imperatives

We must work diligently in the pursuit of holiness.[82] First, our effort must be Spirit-empowered in that the Holy Spirit exposes sin so we can see it and avoid it (John 16:7–11); the Spirit illumines the Word so we can understand and apply it (1 Cor 2:6–16); and the Spirit takes the veil away so we can see the glory of Christ (John 16:14). Second, our effort must be gospel-driven in that the gospel encourages godliness out of a sense of gratitude for what Christ has done (Rom 12:1–2) and aids our pursuit of holiness by telling us about who we are (Col 3:1–4). Third, our effort

78. Jones, *Antinomianism*, 84–87. Jones discusses the distinction between the "benevolent" love of God, which is bestowed on the elect apart from any virtue in them, and the "complacent" love of God, which is bestowed on those whom God approves because they obey his commands. This twofold distinction of God's love is affirmed by "literally dozens of highly regarded Reformed theologians from the Reformation and post-Reformation" (85). See n146 in chapter 6 above for more explanation of God's complacent love.

79. Jones, *Antinomianism*, 86.

80. For example, Haskins et al., *Pilgrim's Guide to Rest*, 125: "Paul never offers sanctification as the measuring stick of God's pleasure toward us."

81. Jones, *Antinomianism*, 92–95.

82. Radical Grace's way of resolving the problem of moralistic performancism in the believer's experience of sanctification is to relax, remember, trust, receive, and grow in understanding—all of these ideas clearly falling on the "don't work" side of the activity spectrum (viewing the activity spectrum with "working hard" on one end and "not working at all" on the other end). This lack of emphasis on effort in the Christian life is the failure of the Radical Grace project.

must be faith fueled in that it rests on the promises God makes to His children (Matt 5:3–12).[83]

The Neglect of the Moral Law

The third way Radical Grace has minimized perseverance is in its denial of the third use of the law. As described earlier, the third use of the law was Calvin's way of describing the use of the OT Law as a guide for Christian living.[84] While not every Radical Grace teacher would decry the third use of the law,[85] most agree with Gerhard Forde that the law, when used as God intended, is only for unbelievers.[86] Such a position logically assumes the diminished expectation of persevering obedience in response to God's commands.

RADICAL GRACE: ITS COMPARISON TO ANTINOMIANISM

I agree with Mark Jones regarding many subtle similarities between Radical Grace teaching in our day and the antinomianism of the seventeenth century. We will look at these five similarities before providing a summary of how Radical Grace theology intersects with the six characteristics of Antinomianism provided at the end of chapter 6.

Jones has helpfully organized the observations of Puritan theologian Anthony Burgess (1600–1664) about the antinomian controversy of his day into five themes.[87] First, we must be careful not to exalt preaching about grace that overshadows the centrality of Christ. "There is today a great deal of talk about 'grace.' It is described as scandalous, liberating, shocking, counterintuitive, unpredictable, dangerous, etc. But when an emphasis on grace eclipses a focus on Christ . . . then grace is not being preached."[88]

Second, oftentimes antinomians reject the accusation of antinomianism in their writings, but in the end they are "loath to speak about

83. DeYoung, *Holiness*, 81–88.
84. See n12.
85. Jon Moffitt and Justin Perdue of Theocast do affirm Calvin's third use as legitimate for believers. See "Intro to Three Uses of the Law," Theocast, https://www.theocastcommunity.org/c/theocast/intro-to-three-uses-of-the-law, accessed December 30, 2024.
86. Forde, *Christ and the Christian Life*, 201–11; Zahl, *Low Anthropology*, 192–94.
87. Jones, *Antinomianism*, 114–18. See Anthony Burgess, *Vindiciae legis: or, A vindication of the morall law and the covenants, from the Errours of Papists, Arminians, Socinians, and more especially Antinomians* (London: Thomas Underhill, 1647).
88. Jones, *Antinomianism*, 114.

the moral law in a positive sense,"[89] and they actually end up supporting antinomian ideas as they proceed.[90] Tchividjian's exegesis of Philippians 2:12–13 illustrates this point: "Think of what Paul tells us in Philippians 2:12: 'Work out your own salvation with fear and trembling.' We've got work to do—but what exactly is it? Get better? Try harder? Pray more? Get more involved in church? Read the Bible longer? What *precisely* is Paul exhorting us to do? He goes on to explain: 'For it is God who works in you, both to will and to work for his good pleasure' (v. 13). God works *his* work in *you*, which is the work already accomplished by Christ. Our hard work, therefore, means coming to a greater understanding of his work."[91]

Third, antinomians tend to preach texts that speak of Christ and his grace but then avoid those texts that command duties and commend God's law. The antidote for this tendency is why we commend expositional preaching at our seminaries: we must preach the whole counsel of God (Acts 20:27; 2 Tim 4:2)! Jones notes, "Frequently, antinomians are in more serious error in what they fail to say than in what they do say."[92]

Fourth, antinomians tend to speak as though they have discovered some grand new truth, some "better" way. "The rhetoric one often hears today has to do with 'getting it.' That someone 'gets grace' often really means that 'it does not matter what we do.' Condescending talk abounds from the lips of modern-day antinomians who think they alone understand what grace is."[93]

Fifth, the antinomian tends to become very repetitious in his sermons, preaching grace and gospel, all the while thinking that the same point must be made in every sermon. Do you have problems in your marriage? Believe the gospel. Do you struggle with pornography? Believe the gospel. Do you have an anxiety problem? Believe the gospel. Jones comments, "One of the dangers of antinomian preaching: it becomes boring. The same repetitive mantras are preached week after week, to the point that if you have heard one sermon, you have heard them all. . . . Christ should

89. Jones, *Antinomianism*, 115.
90. One example is Gerhard Forde, who is critiqued well by Kilcrease, "Gerhard Forde's Doctrine of Law," 164–69.
91. Tchividjian, *Jesus + Nothing*, 96 (emphases original). Jones, *Antinomianism*, 116, comments, "How does this fit with Paul's exhortation to work out our salvation with fear and trembling? Paul surely did not reduce Christian living to contemplating Christ."
92. Jones, *Antinomianism*, 117.
93. Jones, *Antinomianism*, 117.

be in every sermon, as we see in apostolic example and teaching. Preaching the whole Christ prevents us from becoming monotonous in our so-called gospel summaries at the end of every sermon."[94]

While Jones certainly saw many similarities between writers like Forde and Tchividjian and seventeenth-century antinomianism, he wrote before anything like an identifiable group of antinomian thinkers (e.g., Radical Grace) could be circumscribed.[95] He mentioned these five antinomian themes before the Liberate Conference was in full swing and before the existence of Theocast, Mockingbird, or 1517.org. And yet, he did help make the comparison to antinomian theologians of the past, paving the way for us to make connections between Radical Grace theology and antinomianism.

There are a number of connections between Radical Grace writings and the six antinomian characteristics given in our historical survey in chapter 6. First, several teachers ignore or greatly minimize the function of the moral law in the Christian's life. Whether through denial of the third use of the law or the denigration of the imperatives as unwanted duties for the believer, these teachers support characteristic 1 of antinomianism. Second, stressing the indicatives while minimizing the imperatives (characteristic 3) is a well-attested quality of Radical Grace teaching as seen in the rest/relax language that so many use.

Third, characteristic 4 (blurring the differences between justification and sanctification) makes a frequent appearance in Radical Grace literature as the monergism of justification (that God alone justifies apart from any works by the human being) is also applied to sanctification, which should be understood as a synergistic work (Phil 2:12–13). Fourth, several Radical Grace proponents emphasize that the only basis for assurance is the promises of God and that obedience of life cannot be used for this purpose (characteristic 5).

To summarize, we have noted that Radical Grace teaching intersects with four of the six main characteristics of antinomian doctrine delineated in chapter 6. Hence, we have included Radical Grace theology as one of the current-day erroneous distortions of perseverance, and it is a doctrine that should be recognized for what it represents—a great danger to the church.

94. Jones, *Antinomianism*, 118.
95. Jones, *Antinomianism*, 123–30, written in 2013.

CHAPTER 9

HYPER-GRACE AND PERSEVERANCE

INTRODUCTION

I have likened part 2 of this book to an excursion down the Antinomian River. Thus far our trip has included a journey through the past in chapter 6 as we surveyed the various points in church history when antinomian teaching sprang up. That foray into the world of antinomian thought revealed six characteristics that have provided the glasses through which we can view the modern permutations of antinomianism in the evangelical church.

As our ship has continued down the river into the present day, we have encountered three tributaries of grace entering the river. In chapter 7 we learned that the first of these streams goes by the name of Free Grace and that its source was the Chaferian model of sanctification. Flowing out of the Reformed model of sanctification a second grace stream called Radical Grace bubbled into the Antinomian River, and we studied this tributary in chapter 8.

And now our ship has sailed into the flow of a third stream of teaching called Hyper-Grace. But just as the Free Grace and Radical Grace streams had different sources, the same is true of Hyper-Grace, and its headwaters is the Pentecostal model of sanctification.[1]

Before commencing our study of Hyper-Grace, one further comparison with the other two streams should be helpful, and this relates to the foundational motive behind each of these grace

1. Portions of this chapter were first published as Jonathan Pratt, "Hyper-Grace and Perseverance," *DBSJ* 28 (2023): 65–80. Used with permission. For explanation of the Pentecostal model of sanctification see Stanley M. Horton, "The Pentecostal Perspective," in Dieter, *Five Views on Sanctification*, 103–35; and Russell P. Spittler, "The Pentecostal View," in Alexander, *Christian Spirituality*, 133–54.

groups. Free Grace teachers deny perseverance because of their desire to give believers absolute assurance of salvation, for if believers' assurance is threatened by their disobedience, then they become ineffective in their Christian witness and testimony. Regarding Radical Grace theology, a specific foundation is not so readily apparent as it is for Free Grace defenders. It appears that the Lutheran distinction between Law and Gospel and how this distinction should be applied to both justification and sanctification stands as the best explanation for Radical Grace antinomianism. Determining the motivation behind grace teaching in the Hyper-Grace camp is quite difficult. One of the most critical voices of the Hyper-Grace message is Michael Brown,[2] and he suggests that the legalistic tendencies of the holiness-sanctification teachers who birthed Pentecostalism may have created the legalistic environment out of which antinomianism was destined to rise.[3] With few alternative explanations at hand, the idea of a reaction against legalistic holiness emphases makes good sense.

With these distinctions in mind we turn to a study of the Hyper-Grace movement. First, I provide a history of the group, detailing its proponents and their writings. Second, I delineate the tenets of Hyper-Grace teaching. Third, I evaluate how Hyper-Grace theology relates to the doctrine of perseverance. And finally, I seek to show how Hyper-Grace intersects with antinomianism in order to show that it deserves a place on the map of the Antinomian River.

THE HISTORY OF HYPER-GRACE

The Theological Home of Hyper-Grace

As already stated above, Hyper-Grace teaching arises out of the Pentecostal model of sanctification, and all of its supporters fall under the theological umbrella of Pentecostalism. But how should we define the Pentecostal movement? Allan Anderson helpfully narrows down

---

2. Michael L. Brown, *Hyper-Grace* (Lake Mary, FL: Charisma House, 2014) is the best book-length critique of Hyper-Grace to date.
3. Michael L. Brown, personal email to the author, July 11, 2022 (used with permission). Also see Trevor Grizzle, "The Hyper-Grace Gospel," in *The Truth about Grace*, ed. Vinson Synan (Lake Mary, FL: Charisma House, 2018), 32, who writes, "Hyper-grace Christianity emerged largely in reaction to a legalistic religion that eviscerated the life-giving gospel, corroded and toxified Christianity, and brought people under the thralldom of rules and regulations that were impossible to keep and resulted only in spiritual death."

Pentecostal identity into two characteristics: (1) they believe in the *experience* of receiving the baptism of the Holy Spirit subsequent to salvation, and (2) they believe that Christians should *practice* all the spiritual gifts.[4] Some may quibble over such a truncated description of Pentecostalism, but all Hyper-Grace teachers would hold to these two main features.

The History and Proponents of Hyper-Grace

Please note the main teachers and writings of Hyper-Grace as we look at its historical underpinnings. The "movement's most prominent voice" is Singapore pastor Joseph Prince.[5] He has twenty-eight published books to his name; those which proclaim the Hyper-Grace message most specifically are *Destined to Reign*, *Unmerited Favor*, *The Power of Right Believing*, and *Grace Revolution*.[6]

The next two authors have been writing about grace since the 1990s. Steve McVey, originally a pastor and now leader of Grace Walk Ministries, has written *Grace Walk* and *The Secret of Grace*.[7] Rob Rufus, who

---

4. Allan Anderson, *An Introduction to Pentecostalism*, 2nd ed. (Cambridge: Cambridge University Press, 2014), 6; idem, "Varieties, Taxonomies, and Definitions," in *Studying Global Pentecostalism: Theories and Methods*, ed. Allan Anderson et al. (Los Angeles: University of California Press, 2010), 25; Robert Mapes Anderson, *Vision of the Disinherited: The Making of American Pentecostalism* (New York: Oxford University Press, 1979), 4. Walter J. Hollenweger, *Pentecostalism: Origins and Developments Worldwide* (Peabody, MA: Hendrickson, 1997), 327, clarifies the second point by suggesting that Pentecostals do not merely believe in the experience or continuation of the charismata but also agree that they should be demonstrated in the church. Donald W. Dayton, *Theological Roots of Pentecostalism* (Metuchen, NJ: Scarecrow Press, 1987), 20–21, argues for a fourfold definition that includes salvation, subsequent Spirit baptism, practice of physical healing, and anticipation of the second coming of Jesus.

   Entire books have been written on the history and definition of Pentecostalism as a movement, but here are three places one could begin such a study: Vinson Synan, *The Holiness-Pentecostal Tradition: Charismatic Movements in the Twentieth Century*, 2nd ed. (Grand Rapids: Eerdmans, 1997), 279–98; Jonathan Black, *40 Questions About Pentecostalism* (Grand Rapids: Kregel Academic, 2024), 15–52; and Anderson, "Varieties, Taxonomies, and Definitions," 17–20.
5. This is the opinion of Grizzle, "Hyper-Grace Gospel," 34, but based on the popularity of Prince's many published books (most Hyper-Grace authors are self-published while most of Prince's books are not), the church he pastors (New Creation Church has 31,000 attendees), and his daily TV broadcast, *Destined to Reign*, it is an accurate assessment.
6. Joseph Prince, *Destined to Reign* (Tulsa, OK: Harrison House, 2007); idem, *Unmerited Favor* (Lake Mary, FL: Charisma House, 2011); idem, *The Power of Right Believing* (New York: Faith Words, 2013); idem, *Grace Revolution* (New York: Faith Words, 2015).
7. Steve McVey, *Grace Walk* (Eugene, OR: Harvest House, 1995) and *The Secret of Grace* (Eugene, OR: Harvest House, 2014). This second book is a revised and updated version of *Grace Rules* (Eugene, OR: Harvest House, 1998). McVey's website (gracewalk.org)

retired in 2022 from a seventeen-year ministry as pastor of City Church International in Hong Kong, has written *Living in the Grace of God*.[8]

Clark Whitten has pastored for forty-five years; he has led three megachurches and started his current church, Grace Church, in Longwood, Florida, in 2005. His book, *Pure Grace: The Life Changing Power of Uncontaminated Grace*, is one of the clearest explanations of Hyper-Grace teaching available.[9] Paul Ellis maintains the most up-to-date website on the Hyper-Grace movement, and he has also written two books that are well-known in Hyper-Grace circles.[10]

Next, Andrew Wommack's two contributions to Hyper-Grace teaching (*Living in the Balance of Grace & Faith* and *Grace, the Power of the Gospel*) are only a small part of his larger ministry.[11] He founded Charis Bible College in 1994, hosts a daily TV show called *Gospel Truth TV*, and directs the Truth and Liberty Coalition, a politically conservative think tank. Andrew Farley pastors The Grace Church in Lubbock, Texas, and has published nine books in support of the Hyper-Grace message. His most significant titles are *The Naked Gospel* (2009) and *The Grace Message* (2022).[12]

A number of other authors have contributed to the huge body of Hyper-Grace literature in the past fifteen years. The ability to self-publish has likely been a major reason for the plethora of these books. I list them here without further comment: Kevin Ashwe,[13]

---

does not appear to have been updated since 2017. See https://stevemcvey.com/, accessed December 31, 2024.

8. Rob Rufus, *Living in the Grace of God* (London: Authentic Books, 1997). See his website: https://robrufusministries.com/, accessed December 31, 2024.
9. Clark Whitten, *Pure Grace: The Life Changing Power of Uncontaminated Grace* (Shippensburg, PA: Destiny Image Publishers, 2012).
10. See https://escapetoreality.org/, accessed December 31, 2024. Paul Ellis, *The Gospel in Ten Words* (Birkenhead, New Zealand: KingsPress, 2012); idem, *The Hyper-Grace Gospel: A Response to Michael Brown and Those Opposed to the Modern Grace Message* (Birkenhead, New Zealand: KingsPress, 2014).
11. See https://www.awmi.net/, accessed December 31, 2024. Andrew Wommack, *Living in the Balance of Grace & Faith: Combining Two Powerful Forces to Receive from God* (Tulsa, OK: Harrison House, 2009); idem, *Grace, the Power of the Gospel: It's Not What You Do but What Jesus Did* (Tulsa, OK: Harrison House, 2007).
12. Andrew Farley, *The Naked Gospel: The Truth You May Never Hear in Church* (Grand Rapids: Zondervan Academic, 2009); idem, *The Grace Message* (Washington, DC: Salem Books, 2022). See his website, https://andrewfarley.org/, accessed December 31, 2024.
13. Kevin Ashwe, *Should Christians Confess Sins? Effortless Deliverance from the Bondage of Sin Consciousness* (Kindle edition, 2021); Kevin Ashwe, *Why I Don't Preach Sin: What Was Jesus Preaching that Attracted Sinners to Him? What Are We Preaching Today That Keeps Sinners Away from Church?* (Kindle edition, 2020).

Chuck Crisco,[14] Ryan Haley,[15] Ralph Harris,[16] Zach Maldonado,[17] Matt McMillen,[18] D. R. Silva,[19] Eddie Snipes,[20] and André van der Merwe.[21]

These writings have several characteristics in common. First, they are in solid agreement with Hyper-Grace teaching, sounding the same themes again and again. Second, many of the authors endorse each other's books. Third, sixteen of the twenty-eight books cited here are self-published, seven are (understandably) published by Pentecostal printers, and the remaining five are from well-known publishers like Zondervan, Salem Books (an imprint of Regnery), and Harvest House. Fourth, all of these authors are either pastors, former pastors, overseers of Christian organizations, or lay people; none have earned doctorates in biblical or theological studies.[22] Fifth, none of these books have a Scripture index.

Up to this point I have referred at least twice to Hyper-Grace teaching without giving any description of its content, so next we consider the content of Hyper-Grace teaching.

---

14. Chuck Crisco, *Extraordinary Gospel: Experiencing the Goodness of God* (Travelers Rest, SC: True Potential, 2013).
15. Ryan Haley, *A Better Way: God's Design for Less Stress, More Rest, and Greater Success* (Fresno, CA: Ignite Press, 2020).
16. Ralph Harris, *God's Astounding Opinion of You: Understanding Your Identity Will Change Your Life* (Eugene, OR: Harvest House, 2007); Ralph Harris, *Life According to Perfect: The Greatest Story Never Imagined* (N.p., 2018).
17. Zach Maldonado, *Perfect and Forgiven: Discovering Your Freedom from Shame, Guilt, and Sin* (pub. by author, 2019); idem, *The Cross Worked: Why You Can Have Confidence on the Day of Judgment* (pub. by author, 2018).
18. Matt McMillen, *The Christian Identity: Discovering What Jesus Has Truly Done to Us*, 3 vols (Farmington, MO: Matt McMillen Ministries, 2018–2020).
19. D. R. Silva, *Hyper-Grace: The Dangerous Doctrine of a Happy God* (Havre, MT: Up-Arrow Publishing, 2014).
20. Eddie Snipes, *Abounding Grace: Dispelling Myths and Clarifying the Biblical Message of God's Overflowing Grace* (Carrollton, GA: GES Book Publishing, 2013).
21. Andre van der Merwe, *Grace, the Forbidden Gospel* (Bloomington, IN: WestBow, 2011).
22. Lest readers think that Pentecostalism has no one trained in biblical and theological studies, they should know that Hyper-Grace teaching has been addressed extensively by several well-trained Pentecostal theologians. For example, Michael Brown, who wrote *Hyper-Grace*, has a PhD in Near Eastern Languages and Literature; Vinson Synan, ed., *The Truth About Grace* (Lake Mary, FL: Charisma House, 2018) was the premier Pentecostal historian with a PhD in American Social & Intellectual History before he died in 2020. He gathered seventeen contributors for this book, all but three of whom have earned doctorates. Joseph Mattera has a DMin and writes about many topics, including Hyper-Grace (https://josephmattera.org/). Finally, David Kowalski, whose articles appear on Apologetics Index (https://www.apologeticsindex.org/), has an MA and has written extensively on the Hyper-Grace movement; see "The Modern 'Grace Message'—Revolution or Rebellion?," Apologetics Index, December 3, 2014, https://www.apologeticsindex.org/4981-antinomianism, for an excellent critique of Hyper-Grace.

THE TEACHING OF HYPER-GRACE

Six Major Themes of Hyper-Grace Writings

We will first ponder six major themes found in Hyper-Grace literature. I have limited the number of supporting citations, but the reader can be assured that there are many more authors who could be referenced as we proceed through each theme. Following this survey I provide biblical responses to each of these Hyper-Grace concepts.

God Has Already Forgiven All Our Sins

Joseph Prince writes, "You will only love Jesus much when you experience His lavish grace and unmerited favor in forgiving you of all your sins—past, present and future. . . . Beloved, with one sacrifice on the cross, Jesus blotted out all the sins of your entire life!"[23] Andrew Farley concurs: "Our past, present, and future sins were dealt with simultaneously through the cross."[24] While these statements sound orthodox, Hyper-Grace teachers go beyond this truth (see 2 John 9) and purport that there are several amazing effects in the life of the believer.

First, there is no need to confess our sins to God because they have already been forgiven.[25] Hyper-Grace teachers respond to the two texts most commonly put forward by objectors in this manner: (1) Matthew 6:12 states that we should seek forgiveness for our sins, but this verse was given under the old covenant, and now that believers are under the new covenant and its promise of forgiveness, believers need not seek forgiveness;[26] (2) 1 John 1:9 talks about confession, but this is actually talking about the need for unbelievers to confess their sins so that they can be saved.[27]

---

23. Prince, *Unmerited Favor*, 194–95.
24. Farley, *Naked Gospel*, 145.
25. Whitten, *Pure Grace*, 94, writes, "You are not required to confess your sin to God in order to be forgiven ever again. You already are forgiven." Ellis, *Hyper-Grace Gospel*, 33, understands the word "confess" to mean "receiving grace" and states, "Receiving grace is simply a matter of agreeing with God. It's thanking Him that through Jesus 'I have been cleansed from all unrighteousness, and all my sins have been taken away.'"
26. McVey, *Secret of Grace*, 135–38, explains, "Under the Covenant of Law, a person was not totally forgiven. He or she had to receive ongoing forgiveness in order to remain in a guilt-free state. But at the cross, God poured out all His forgiveness on us. We don't need to ask for more!"
27. Whitten, *Pure Grace*, 94, "First John 1:9 does not say that a Christian must confess sins to God in order to be forgiven. . . . This verse is not directed toward believers, but toward those who need salvation." Also see Farley, *Naked Gospel*, 152, "Verse 9 is a remedy for

A second effect of being forgiven is that the Holy Spirit does not convict believers of sin because God has forgiven and "still sees [the Christian] as righteous."[28]

Third, a change of behavior as a fruit of repentance is not expected since repentance is viewed only as a change of mind; it does not refer to sorrow for sin nor to a change of behavior.[29]

Imbalance of Teaching Between Position and Practice in Sanctification

Hyper-Grace literature places strong emphasis on position accompanied by an equally strong deemphasis on practice. For example: "The core of the Christian life doesn't revolve around *doing*, but is grounded in *being*. . . . As we experience the law of the Spirit of life in Christ Jesus, godly action is the consequence of His life flowing from us. It is not the result of dedicated effort on our part."[30] "You are like Him, my friend, and are in a permanent and unchangeable state of being of holiness."[31]

---

unbelievers who have been influenced by Gnostic peer pressure and are now claiming sinless perfection."

28. Prince, *Destined to Reign*, 134–35. He also states, "The bottom line is that the Holy Spirit never convicts you of your sins. He NEVER comes to point out your faults. I challenge you to find a Scripture in the Bible that tells you that the Holy Spirit has come to convict you of your sins" (emphasis original). Also Whitten, *Pure Grace*, 106: "In reality, there are not many biblical references to support the concept that the Holy Spirit's primary ministry is to convict believers of sin. As a matter of fact, there are no New Testament verses that refer to the concept!"
29. Prince, *Destined to Reign*, 233: "Because we have been influenced by our denominational background as well as our own religious upbringing, many of us have the impression that repentance is something that involves mourning and sorrow. However, that is not what the Word of God says. Repentance just means changing your mind." Whitten, *Pure Grace*, 98: "[Repentance] essentially means to rethink your position in light of truth, or change your mind based on the fact that you thought wrongly before and need to embrace the truth of a matter."
30. McVey, *Grace Walk*, 88 (emphasis original).
31. Whitten, *Pure Grace*, 166. Furthermore, "I am already justified, and get this—I am already sanctified! Sanctification—having been made perfect—is a state of being, not a goal to be achieved or grow into. . . . The old religious approach of 'I *am* justified, I *am being* sanctified, and I *will be* glorified' is a lie. It is religious nonsense. Progressive sanctification is based on the theory that we can act better and better until we get to be almost like Jesus on earth, then be fully made perfect in Heaven. . . . God will not do anything to me in Heaven that He hasn't already done here!" (29–30; emphasis in original). See also Prince, *Destined to Reign*, 27: "You are either righteous or you are not. There is no such thing as first having 'positional righteousness' and then having to maintain that through 'practical righteousness.' You are the righteousness of God in Christ, period!"

God Sees Christians as Perfect

Since Hyper-Grace teachers emphasize the position of the believer, they draw attention to God's perception of the Christian. And how does God view his children? "When God looks at me, He doesn't see me through the blood of Christ, He sees me—cleansed! Likewise, He sees us as holy and righteous."[32] And because God views His children as completely righteous and perfect, believers should not try to please God. As Clark Whitten reminds us, "If you are 'working' to please Him, you are in for a lifetime of unfinished business, and it will leave you perpetually exhausted!"[33]

Spirituality Is an Effortless Experience in the Believer's Life

Since legalism is Hyper-Grace's greatest perceived enemy,[34] Hyper-Grace teachers avoid any exhortations to fight sin, seeing them as tools that place rules above relationship.[35] The solution in the battle against legalism is not diligent, Spirit-fueled effort, but it is rather a type of quietism.[36] Christians are called to "focus on our newness and Christ's presence within us" in order to see behavior changed.[37] "There is nothing for you to do, nothing for you to perform, nothing for you to accomplish. . . . Your part in the new covenant is just to have faith in Jesus and to believe that you are totally forgiven and free to enjoy the new covenant blessings through His finished work!"[38] "When you are planted in the fertile soil of God's Word and His grace, fruits of righteousness will manifest effortlessly out of your relationship with Him."[39] Ultimately, these ideas fall under the umbrella of "rest," an idea

32. Whitten, *Pure Grace*, 53. Also, "If you are a true Christian, a believer in Christ, one who has been born again, you are righteous, you are in right standing with God, and absolutely nothing can change that. You are as righteous as Christ is righteous" (50). Paul Ellis, *Hyper-Grace Gospel*, 83, "Your Father loves you 100 percent and is thoroughly pleased with you. He never changes His mind. Just as your behavior does not alter the sunlight falling on the earth, your behavior cannot alter the white-hot love of your Father for you."
33. Whitten, *Pure Grace*, 40.
34. McVey, *Grace Walk*, 80. Whitten, *Pure Grace*, 20, "Legalistic Christianity is in the sin management business full-time and failing miserably at the job. . . . 'Do good, God is glad; do bad, God is mad' is the M.O. of legalistic Christianity."
35. Prince, *Unmerited Favor*, 41.
36. Kevin DeYoung, *The Hole in Our Holiness* (Wheaton, IL: Crossway, 2012), 79–91.
37. Farley, *Naked Gospel*, 208. Also, Andrew Farley, *Relaxing with God: The Neglected Spiritual Discipline* (Grand Rapids: Baker Books, 2014), writes an entire book based on this concept.
38. Prince, *Unmerited Favor*, 177.
39. Prince, *The Power of Right Believing*, 204.

that virtually all Hyper-Grace teachers emphasize as they appeal to Jesus's words, "Come to me, all who labor and are heavy laden, and I will give you rest" (Matt 11:28).[40]

Sin Is Minimized

While there is a woeful lack of discussion about sin in Hyper-Grace literature, we can gain a glimpse into the perspective that many Hyper-Grace teachers possess with regard to sin by noting some of their comments about it. For example, Clark Whitten states, "Christians are truly free. We are free to laugh or cry, read a novel or the Bible, eat meat offered to idols or avoid it, drink wine or water, smoke or chew, get fat or fit, attend church or stay at home, tithe or give nothing—all without condemnation from God."[41] D. R. Silva shares this perspective: "Jesus didn't go around picking on sinners and telling them to quit sinning 'because the Ten Commandments say so!'"[42] And since Jesus destroyed sin on the cross, "sin isn't the issue anymore. More often the issue is the believer's [*sic*] perspective whenever they live as if He didn't deal with sin, thinking they are still 'prone' to it when Paul said to 'consider yourselves dead to it.'"[43]

Devaluation of the Old Testament and the Moral Value of the Law for Believers Today

Many Hyper-Grace instructors emphasize the significance of the institution of the new covenant by Christ in his death, claiming that it has totally replaced the OT law. Consequently, even the teaching of Christ is seen as belonging to the old covenant and applying to only Jewish people, especially when he speaks favorably about the law.[44] In regard

40. Wommack, *Living in the Balance of Grace and Faith*, 76: "God, by grace, has provided everything that is necessary for you to accomplish what He wants you to do. It's already been done. Now you must simply rest and trust that God has already provided everything you need. That sounds easy, but the hardest thing you'll ever do is rest." Also, McVey, *Grace Walk*, 73–74.
41. Whitten, *Pure Grace*, 22. He also writes (20), "My bad works don't move God any more than my good works move Him. He simply isn't moved by 'works' of any kind. If you are motivated to do a great work for God, good luck!"
42. Silva, *Hyper-Grace*, 29.
43. Silva, *Hyper-Grace*, 29.
44. Farley, *Naked Gospel*, 84–86. Two statements from these pages strain credulity: "We often attempt to apply directly to our lives every word Jesus said, without considering his audience and purpose. But the context of Jesus' harsh teachings must be seen in the light of the dividing line between the Old and the New. Remember that Christ was born and

to the moral value of the law, Hyper-Grace teachers are adamantly opposed to any application of the law to the church because law takes away from grace.[45] Clark Whitten exclaims, "The greatest constraining power against sin is love, not law! We were designed to abide in Him and bear much fruit. I am not under the law and never will be again."[46]

While all six of these themes are replete throughout Hyper-Grace literature, the emphasis on *identity* as completely forgiven (1), on *activity* as totally resting (4), and on *relationship* as entirely under the grace of the new covenant (6) are clearly the most important. Next we proceed to a critique of each of these themes.

Scriptural Critique of Hyper-Grace Theology

In a shotgun manner, I will provide succinct critiques to each of the major themes of the Hyper-Grace message.[47]

First, 1 John 1:9 clearly shows that Christians should confess their sins in order to receive forgiveness not for salvation but for fellowship. From 1 John 1:5–2:2 the apostle is providing a series of three contrasts between orthodox believers and false teachers who have been leaving (1 John 2:19), and 1:9 describes the kind of behavior true Christians

lived during the Old Covenant (law) era." "Jesus' impossible teachings of 'sell everything, sever body parts if necessary, be perfect like God and surpass the Pharisees with your righteousness' are not *honestly* compatible with salvation as a gift from God. Couldn't we resolve all of this by realizing the dividing line in human history? Peter, James, John, and Paul wrote epistles about life under the New Covenant. Years earlier, Jesus was teaching hopelessness under the Old. The audience wasn't the same. The covenant wasn't the same. And the teachings aren't the same" (emphasis original).

45. Prince, *Unmerited Favor*, 111–12, argues that God had originally sought a grace relationship with Israel, but at Sinai Israel chose a different route: "The tragedy of all tragedies occurred for the children of Israel when they responded to God after hearing [his words] at the foot of Mount Sinai. They were proud and did not want the relationship God had envisioned. They wanted to deal with God at arm's length, through impersonal commandments." Prince, *Destined to Reign*, 224–25, makes a similar argument. Since part of Prince's argument here is based on how he reads Hebrew syntax, Michael Brown, *Hyper-Grace*, 195–96, shows how wrongly Prince has interpreted Exod 19:4–6, especially in light of his reference to Hebrew syntax.

46. Whitten, *Pure Grace*, 61.

47. Several critiques of Hyper-Grace have been published by Pentecostal authors. I offer them in order of their value for further study. (1) Brown, *Hyper-Grace*; (2) Synan, *Truth about Grace*; (3) David Kowalski, "The Modern 'Grace Message'"; (4) Joseph Mattera, "8 Signs of 'Hypergrace' Churches," JospehMatttera.org, October 13, 2017, https://josephmattera.org/eight-signs-of-hyper-grace-churches-2/; and (5) Andrew Wilson, "The 'Grace Revolution,' Hyper-Grace, and the Humility of Orthodoxy," Think Theology, January 2, 2013, https://thinktheology.co.uk/blog/article/the_grace_revolution.

demonstrate: a willingness to confess their sins.[48] Furthermore, believers are convicted of sin (John 16:8; 1 Cor 14:24) and should repent, not just in their minds but in their actions (2 Cor 7:8–10; Jas 4:1–6).[49]

Second, the indicatives of salvation that declare the believers' identity and position before God are significant, and just as important are the imperatives that call on believers to bear fruit in persevering faith.[50] Both elements are so frequent in Scripture that they cannot all be listed, but see Philippians 2:12–13 and Jude 21–24 for clear examples.[51]

Third, while Christians are clothed in the righteousness of Christ when they are justified, they still sin and are called to please God multiple times (2 Cor 5:9; Eph 5:10; 1 Thess 2:4; 4:1).[52]

Fourth, we know that there is mystery when it comes to the synergistic work of the Spirit and the Christian in progressive sanctification (1 Cor 15:10), but the NT clearly calls believers to labor in cooperation with the Spirit in their growth (Rom 12:9–21; Phil 2:12; 1 Thess 4:3–12).

Fifth, believers continue to be tempted to sin by the world (Jas 1:27; 4:4), the flesh (Rom 13:14), and the devil (1 Pet 5:8–9). And Christians must fight to defeat sin in their striving for holiness (Heb 12:1, 14).

Sixth, even those Christians who do not hold to Calvin's third use of the law still believe that the OT law is "holy, righteous, and good" (Rom 7:12). Christ and the apostles gave commands for believers to obey, based upon the character of God as revealed in the law, and they expected Christians to obey the law of Christ (1 Cor 9:21; Gal 6:2).[53]

THE RELATION OF HYPER-GRACE TO PERSEVERANCE

After considering the six major themes or tenets of Hyper-Grace theology, the conclusion is quite obvious: Hyper-Grace teaching denies or

48. Colin G. Kruse, *The Letters of John*, PNTC (Grand Rapids: Eerdmans, 2000), 61–75; Stephen S. Smalley, *1, 2, 3 John*, WBC (Nashville: Thomas Nelson, 1984), 27–41.
49. Brown, *Hyper-Grace*, 74–80.
50. McCune, *Systematic Theology*, 3:181, states, "If it is true that a believer *will* persevere, then it is equally true that he *must* persevere" (emphasis original).
51. DeYoung, *Hole in Our Holiness*, 79–91.
52. Jones, *Antinomianism*, 92–95; Brown, *Hyper-Grace*, 120–27.
53. Douglas J. Moo, "The Law of Christ as the Fulfillment of the Law of Moses: A Modified Lutheran View," in *Five Views on Law and Gospel*, ed. Wayne Strickland (Grand Rapids: Zondervan Academic, 1996), 319–76; idem, "The Law of Moses or the Law of Christ," in *Continuity and Discontinuity: Perspectives on the Relationship between the Old and New Testament. Essays in Honor of S. Lewis Johnson Jr.*, ed. John S. Feinberg (Westchester, IL: Crossway, 1988), 203–18, 373–76; and Grizzle, "Hyper-Grace Gospel," 35–47.

at best ignores the doctrine of perseverance. They share many similarities with grace instructors from the other two streams—Free Grace and Radical Grace. Like their Free Grace compatriots, Hyper-Grace advocates limit the meaning of repentance to a mere change of mind and also de-emphasize or deny perseverance.[54] Like Radical Grace, Hyper-Grace despises any connection to law, and both groups make strong appeals to a quietist approach to the Christian life (e.g., trust, believe, relax, and rest).

HYPER-GRACE THEOLOGY AND ANTINOMIANISM

How antinomian is Hyper-Grace theology? Well, when we evaluate Hyper-Grace teaching with the six characteristics of antinomianism given in the summary of the doctrine at the end of chapter 6, we find that Hyper-Grace's emphases find more connection with these antinomian qualities than either Free Grace or Radical Grace. First, the stress on the relegation of the OT law to the period of the old covenant as well as the lack of teaching about sin (and its breaking of God's law) shows that Hyper-Grace intersects with antinomianism and characteristic 1. Indeed, Hyper-Grace fits the classic definition of an antinomian at this very point—a rejection of the role of God's law in the life of the believer.

Hyper-Grace also trumpets its support of characteristic 2: God sees no sin in those who are justified. Additionally, characteristic 3 of antinomianism—stressing the indicatives while denying or minimizing the imperatives—manifests itself time and again in Hyper-Grace teaching. Furthermore, Hyper-Grace theology certainly blurs the differences between justification and sanctification (characteristic 4) with its constant reminders of the believer's position in Christ and the need to rest in this truth.

Finally, Hyper-Grace intersects with antinomianism in its failure to recognize the important distinction between the benevolent and complacent love of God for the Christian (characteristic 6). Statements about the futility of wanting to please God and the declarations of God's unchanging love toward the Christian, whether sinning or not, demonstrate this antinomian point well.

---

54. While the two groups agree on deemphasizing perseverance, they do so for different reasons. Free Grace denies perseverance in order to preserve *assurance* while Hyper-Grace denies perseverance in order to preserve *identity* and *position*.

Compared to the Free Grace and Radical Grace tributaries, the Hyper-Grace stream appears to be the largest contributor to Antinomian River.[55] While Free Grace shared at least two of the characteristics of antinomian theology and Radical Grace synced with four, Hyper-Grace connects with five of the six characteristics. To answer the question raised at the beginning of this subsection, Hyper-Grace is very antinomian—Anne Hutchinson and John Eaton would have become fast friends with this group.[56]

We have come to the end of our historical study in part 2 of this book. In chapter 6 we have learned about the history of antinomianism in the Christian church since the Reformation and up to 1950. Then in chapters 7, 8, and 9 we have studied three modern-day permutations of antinomianism see in the teachings of Free Grace (chapter 7), Radical Grace (chapter 8), and Hyper-Grace (chapter 9). We have seen how antinomian teaching in the evangelical church denies, minimizes, or distorts the Bible's teaching about the doctrine of perseverance. How shall we then live in light of the antinomianism among us? I hope to answer this question in chapter 10.

---

55. This statement is true not only doctrinally but also numerically. While I cannot provide any hard data to support this assertion, I would suggest that since the Hyper-Grace message is connected to Pentecostalism, it is likely affecting far more Christians than Free Grace and Radical Grace combined.
56. Before leaving this discussion about antinomianism among the Pentecostals, I would like to make two final observations: (1) contrary to the claims of some evangelicals (e.g., John MacArthur, *Strange Fire: The Danger of Offending the Holy Spirit with Counterfeit Worship* [Nashville: Nelson Books, 2013], 235, writes, "When notable continuationist scholars give credence to charismatic interpretations or fail to directly condemn charismatic practices, they provide theological cover for a movement that ought to be exposed for its dangers rather than defended."), Pentecostals do critique their own. While they certainly do not criticize themselves regarding continuationism and their doctrine of baptism with the Spirit, they have raised red flags against Hyper-Grace and have usually done so from a much stronger position of exegetical acumen and intellectual rigor than their Hyper-Grace proponents (see n 47).

    (2) It appears that Pentecostalism has at least four significant areas of doctrinal deviation in its ranks, all requiring attention from the more orthodox scholars of the movement: oneness Pentecostalism, Word-Faith/prosperity teaching, the New Apostolic Reformation, and Hyper-Grace. While some have called others to account in Pentecostalism (as seen in this chapter), much more vigilance is needed so that these heterodox elements could be purged from the church and "God would grant them repentance leading to a knowledge of the truth" (2 Tim 2:25).

CONCLUSION

SUMMARY

In John 10:27 Jesus gave one of the most concise statements of perseverance found in the Bible: "My sheep hear my voice, and I know them, and they follow me." These are the words I have chosen as the title for this book, *My Sheep Follow Me*, because true believers persevere in faith and good works to the end of their earthly lives.

Initially, I tried to explain this meaning of perseverance in comparison with two companion doctrines—assurance and preservation/eternal security—so that the reader would not experience a confusion of categories. Then in part 1, I showed how the Bible teaches in clear and no uncertain terms that Jesus (chapter 2), Paul (chapter 3), and the General Epistles (chapter 4) support the doctrine of perseverance in how they speak of the indicatives of sanctification; that is, the declarative statements of believers' continuance in faith and good works to the end of their lives. In addition to this scriptural foundation, I demonstrated *how* the Lord helps to produce perseverance in the Christian life as we considered five means used by the Lord in chapter 5.

Even though John 10:27 and the rest of the biblical support of perseverance provided in part 1 clearly teach the reality of this doctrine, many sanctification teachers have minimized, twisted, or denied the truth of perseverance in the way they have taught about God's grace in the justification and sanctification of the believer. For this reason we needed part 2, where we considered the erroneous distortion of sanctification as seen in the teaching of antinomianism. In particular, the erroneous distortion corresponded with how the imperatives of Scripture were understood by antinomian teachers both in the past and in the present of the evangelical church. We learned that antinomians affirmed the indicatives of sanctification but erroneously distorted the imperatives of sanctification. While both the reality and means of perseverance are taught in Scripture, antinomians want only to emphasize the reality.

So part 2 included a study of antinomianism from 1600–1950 in chapter 6; this short survey generated six particular characteristics of antinomianism that became the basis for studying the modern permutations of antinomianism in the current day:

1. The moral law has no role in the believer's life;
2. God sees no sin in those who are justified;
3. Teaching on sanctification stresses the indicatives and denies or minimizes the imperatives;
4. There is a blurring of the differences between justification and sanctification;
5. Obedience cannot be used as a basis for assurance; and
6. The benevolent and complacent love of God for the Christian are one and the same.

We discovered that three streams of grace teaching have developed in the past fifty years or so, and we learned that each had their headwaters in different sanctification models. In chapter 7 we learned of Free Grace, which was sourced in the Chaferian model. Chapter 8 covered Radical Grace, which flowed from the Reformed model. And in chapter 9 we studied Hyper-Grace, which developed out of the Pentecostal model. Besides noting the different models of sanctification from which each grace group came, we also discovered that each had different motivations behind their dogma: Free Grace—assurance; Radical Grace—law-gospel distinction; and Hyper-Grace—legalistic holiness. Even with these unique distinctives, all three streams in the antinomian river trumpet the same basic grace (antinomian) message.

Our studies of the modern-day antinomians found that each group intersected with the six characteristics of antinomianism in particular ways. As suggested at the end of chapter 6, the various streams of grace teaching do not need to hold to all six of the antinomian characteristics to be considered members of the antinomian club. Rather, likeness in even one area places a group on the antinomian continuum. What did we discover in our study?

1. The moral law has no role in the believer's life.
   - Radical Grace
   - Hyper-Grace
2. God sees no sin in those who are justified.
   - Hyper-Grace
3. Teaching on sanctification stresses the indicatives and denies or minimizes the imperatives.
   - Radical Grace
   - Hyper-Grace
4. There is a blurring of the differences between justification and sanctification.
   - Free Grace
   - Radical Grace
   - Hyper-Grace
5. Obedience cannot be used as a basis for assurance.
   - Free Grace
   - Radical Grace
6. The benevolent and complacent love of God for the Christian are one and the same.
   - Hyper-Grace

Wherever one of the grace teachers lands on the spectrum of antinomianism, being on the grid is a doctrinal problem—one that has significant implications regarding the doctrine of perseverance.

THE IMPLICATIONS OF PERSEVERANCE

My hope in writing this book on the beautiful doctrine of perseverance has been to clarify its meaning, to defend its significance in the biblical record, and to warn of its current-day distortions in evangelical teaching. In what follows I desire to give several ramifications of this book's observations regarding perseverance.

First, while we can marvel at and appreciate the doctrine of perseverance, we must not jettison the Bible's many calls to us to "pursue holiness without which no one will see the Lord" (Heb 12:14).[1] So we must not ignore the imperatives of sanctification. Thus, if it is true that believers will persevere in good works (the indicatives), then it

1. Schreiner, *Run to Win the Prize*, 103.

is equally true that believers must persevere (the imperatives), so we must acknowledge and seek to balance properly both of these truths.[2] Because believers will persevere, we spotlight the indicatives and because believers must persevere, we emphasize the imperatives—whichever is in the text we are studying.

Second, obedience or continuance in the faith is the evidence of true faith, which helps to explain the false faith we sometimes see in the Bible.[3] And it reminds us that false believers are still present and active today in our churches. If they found their way into Ephesus, Colossae, and Crete, and if they found their way into John's churches (1 John 2:19 and Pergamum [Rev 2:12–17] and Thyatira [Rev 2:18–29]), then we should not be surprised if they find their way into ours today. And this truth reminds us to heed the warnings regarding false professors that we see in the NT (2 Tim 2:24–26; 3:1–9; 2 Pet 2:1–22; 1 John 2:18–19; Jude 3–4; Rev 2:14–15, 20–24).

Third, justification and progressive sanctification are connected in such a way that perseverance in good works is an inevitable and necessary result of our justification. Based on this truth, it is not possible to argue for two classes of Christians (the "spiritual" and the "carnal"). To expand on this point: (1) while the NT clearly speaks in regard to the necessity of fruit bearing in the lives of the justified, its authors never suggest that growth in holiness is completed or perfected in the earthly existence of the believer, and the numerous imperatives given to believers calling them to obedience and growth should quickly dispel such thinking; and (2) we all observe various levels or degrees of maturity and growth in the experience of believers, but the NT gives no indication of distinct classes of Christians, nor does it advocate certain types of decisions to help move a Christian out of one class into another.[4]

Fourth, the perseverance texts show that God initiates and brings forth fruit in the believer's life (Phil 2:12–13) and that believers must submit obediently to the Spirit's prompting (Gal 5:16–18). This reminds us again of the *mystery* of spiritual growth—too much emphasis on

2. McCune, *Systematic Theology*, 3:181; Henžel, "'And Grace Will Lead Me Home,'" 31.
3. McCune, *Systematic Theology*, 3:173–77, mentions Judas Iscariot, Simon Magus (Acts 8:9–24), false prophets (Matt 7:22–23; Mark 7:6–7; 2 Pet 2:20–22); false apostles (2 Cor 11:13–15; Rev 2:2); and secessionists (1 John 2:18–19). I would also add the second and third soils in the parable of the soils (Matt 13:5–7, 20–22) and "believers" in John's gospel (John 2:23–25; 8:30, 31, 59).
4. Reisinger, *What Should We Think of "The Carnal Christian"?*

God's work and the indicatives of sanctification and *antinomianism* results, and too much emphasis on man's work and the imperatives of sanctification and *moralism* or *legalism* results. First Corinthians 15:10 expresses this mystery: "But by the grace of God I am what I am, and his grace toward me was not in vain. On the contrary, I worked harder than any of them, though it was not I, but the grace of God that is with me." The best course for avoiding imbalance regarding this mystery is to preach God's Word expositionally and in this way to preach the whole counsel of God (Acts 20:27).[5]

Fifth, there is no need for a jump start, a second work of grace, an act of consecration or dedication, to activate one's spiritual growth. While it is true that some experience a period (or even periods) of spiritual lethargy following their justification only to see a significant jump in their spiritual vitality due to a significant spiritual decision, this is only experiential and should not be presumed as normative for all believers. The doctrine of perseverance shows that the production of spiritual fruit begins at regeneration and continues to the end of life. J. I. Packer was right: "The Christian's motto should not be 'Let go and let God' but 'Trust God and get going!'"[6]

Sixth, in the interests of theological precision, preachers and teachers will be more helpful to their hearers if they make a clear distinction between *perseverance* and *eternal security/preservation*. On the one hand, preachers and teachers should remind believers that God will enable them to continue in faith and good works to the end of their earthly lives (perseverance), and on the other hand, preachers and teachers should remind believers that God ensures they cannot lose their salvation (eternal security/preservation). The latter truth encourages them to stay engaged in the former.

Seventh, I have not called our antinomian grace teachers heretics, because I do not consider them to be teaching false doctrine along the lines of an Arian or modalist. But all the grace streams we have considered need correction because of their antinomian characteristics. Reasons for applying labels like antinomianism to these distorters of perseverance could certainly be varied. Motives could include the

---

5. Mark Dever, *9 Marks of a Healthy Church*, rev ed. (Wheaton, IL: Crossway, 2004), 35–55; Derek W. H. Thomas, "Expository Preaching," in *A Passionate Plea for Preaching*, ed. Don Kistler (Sanford, FL: Reformation Trust, 2008), 35–51.
6. J. I. Packer, *Keep in Step with the Spirit* (Old Tappan, NJ: Fleming H. Revell, 1984), 157.

goal of (a) dismissing them, (b) canceling them, (c) alerting them to the dangerous nature of their teaching, (d) calling them to turn from this wayward path and back onto the road leading to the Celestial City, or (e) warning others about them. My purpose has been to warn the church, to alert the antinomians, and to call them back to a biblical understanding of perseverance. I hope these goals have been accomplished without any hint of dismissal or cancellation.

Eighth, to expand a bit on the motive of warning, I believe that misdirected interpretations of various biblical texts have caused an imbalance in understanding perseverance correctly. Silenced words in regard to holy living, honest repentance, and strenuous effort still speak, and sound eerily similar to Paul's interlocutor in Romans 6:1, "Are we to continue in sin that grace may abound?," and in 6:15, "Are we to sin because we are not under law but under grace?" My answer to these grace teachers is the same as Paul's: "By no means!" May God help us to avoid such antinomian influences, to be balanced in our preaching and teaching by emphasizing both the indicatives and imperatives of Scripture, and to let each passage speak for itself.

I hope that the readers of this book will persevere to the end in faith and good works. I also desire that learning about the antinomian threats to an accurate understanding of perseverance will help to thwart their siren calls to ignore holy living, repentance from sin, and the commands to follow Christ. These hopes are grounded in the truths of the Scripture passages considered in this book, and they form the basis of my prayers for the perseverance of my family members, fellow church members, friends, and members of the seminary community where I teach—this is my circle of people. And I hope that these same truths will increase the prayers for perseverance that every reader of this book can pour out for the friends and relatives in his or her sphere of influence. Prayers like these are biblical, and God will certainly use them to accomplish the good work he is bringing to completion in the lives of his sheep who follow him.

SCRIPTURE INDEX

Acts

Romans

1 Corinthians

2 Corinthians

Galatians

Ephesians

James

1 Peter

2 Peter

1 John

2 John

Jude

Revelation